ESPORTS
THE ULTIMATE GUIDE

SCHOLASTIC

ESPORTS
THE ULTIMATE GUIDE

ISBN: 978-1-338-58054-9

Printed in the U.S.A.   40
First printing, January 2020

Scholastic is constantly working to lessen the environmental impact of our manufacturing processes. To view our industry-leading paper procurement policy, visit www.scholastic.com/paperpolicy.

All statistics, facts, and other information contained in this book are accurate at the time of going to press. Given how fast the world of gaming moves, we can accept no responsibility for things that have changed between writing and publication, but we've done our utmost to make the book as accurate and relevant as it can possibly be.

Copyright: ESL | Helena Kristiansson

STAY SAFE AND HAVE FUN...

Games can be amazing, but it's important that you know how to stay safe when playing online. These ten simple tips will help you to have fun while playing. Follow these and you can have a great time online, while your parents can rest easy in the knowledge that you know how to stay safe.

1. Discuss and agree on rules with your parents regarding how long you can stay online, what websites you can visit on the internet, and what apps and games you can use.
2. Remember to take frequent breaks during gaming sessions.
3. Never give out personal information such as passwords, your real name, phone number, or anything about your parents.
4. Never agree to meet in person with someone you've met online.
5. Tell your parents or a teacher if you come across anything online that makes you feel uncomfortable, upset, or scared.
6. Whenever you're online, be nice to other people and players. Never say or do anything that might hurt someone else's feelings or make them feel sad.
7. Pay attention to age ratings on games. They exist for a reason—to help protect you from any inappropriate content, not to stop you from having fun!
8. Don't download or install software or apps to any device, or fill out any forms on the internet, without first checking with the person who owns the device you're using.
9. If you play mobile games outside, be aware of your surroundings at all times, and don't play alone—always have a friend or family member with you.
10. When using streaming services, always check with an adult before changing to a different video or game.

CONTENTS

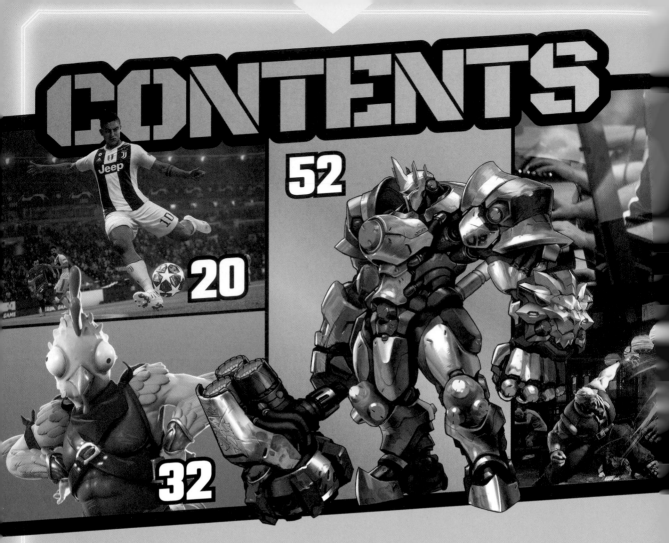

52

20

32

GAME FOCUS

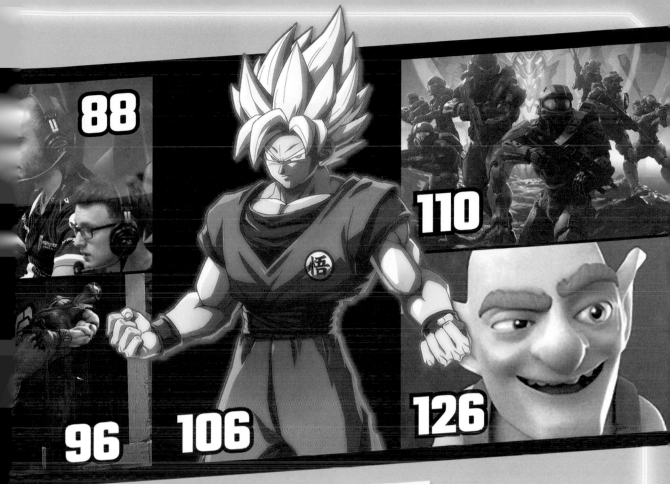

88

110

96 **106**

126

WHAT ARE ESPORTS?

DISCOVER THE WORLD OF COMPETITIVE GAMING!

Nowadays, a computer game isn't just something that you play by yourself. Every week, hundreds of thousands of viewers tune in to watch the most talented gamers in the world compete with each other in every imaginable way, from football fields to card tables, fantastical realms to laser-scarred sci-fi battlefields. This is esports—a world of high-stakes digital competition where millions of dollars can be won (or lost) based on split-second decision-making, teamwork, and skill. It's a new form of competitive entertainment that has won over millions of fans in a few short decades—and it's only getting bigger!

The esports scene has grown from humble origins. In the 1980s and 1990s, competitive gaming was a hobby shared by many, but it was limited by the need to travel to arcades, computer events called "LAN parties," and a few small tournaments held around the world. The rapid rise of the internet changed all that. Starting in the 2000s, it became much easier for players all across the globe to get access to a gaming computer and a fast internet café. In North America and Europe, players started competing with one another online by the thousands, eventually forming professional teams to compete for prize money and esteem. Esports grew even more

ESPORTS HISTORY

THE RISE OF A NEW KIND OF COMPETITION

▶ **ARCADE ORIGINS**
In the 1970s and 1980s, one-off tournaments and gameshow-style competitions grow in popularity.

▶ **VERSUS MODE**
The rise of fighting games and FPS titles in the 1990s help make competitive gaming more popular.

▶ **GOING GLOBAL**
Faster internet speeds help make online competitive gaming a hit!

quickly in Asia, where internet cafés rapidly became a hotbed for top-level competitive play, and the best gamers quickly found themselves turning into celebrities.

Since then, esports have grown into a worldwide industry. Around the world, fans file into sports stadiums and convention centers in the thousands to watch nail-biting contests of skill, while millions more view the action via online livestreams. The best gamers in the world understand the games they play at a deep level, and watching talented pros demonstrate their ability is one of the biggest thrills in gaming—even though you're not the one playing!

In addition to the players themselves, the esports scene includes commentators and analysts, livestream hosts, camera operators, event organizers, managers, coaches, designers, and many more. Putting on a modern esports event is a team effort

MAJOR PLAYERS

MLG
This veteran US esports organization has run top-tier events for decades.

ESL
Based in Germany, ESL runs stadium-filling tournaments around the world!

DREAMHACK

DREAMHACK
These major LAN events are a cornerstone of competitive gaming on PC.

▶ **RISE OF STREAMING**
Online streaming services, like Twitch, create a huge new audience for esports!

▶ **STADIUM-FILLERS**
As esports continue to grow, more and more stadium events appear around the world!

that involves people from every walk of life, and the industry is always growing to include new disciplines. Even if you don't aspire to one day lift a trophy yourself, chances are that there's a way you could get involved—whether that's leading a discussion on a livestreamed panel, putting together a dramatic stage design for a live event, or helping a team prepare for a major match behind the scenes.

In addition to prize money, some professional gamers earn a salary as part of a competitive gaming organization or esports league.

STATS

$100 MILLION
▶ IN PRIZES AT THE 2019 FORTNITE WORLD CUP

55 GAMES HAVE AWARDED $1M OR MORE

1.9M LIVE VIEWERS FOR THE 2018 LEAGUE OF LEGENDS FINAL!

Others use their talent to draw in sponsors, just like traditional athletes. Also like other athletes, esports players are expected to train hard, take care of themselves, and build a good relationship with their teammates. In the world of competitive gaming, natural talent can only take you so far: It takes serious hard work to rise to the top and win those eye-catching first place prizes!

Ask any pro gamer, however, and they'll tell you that prize money and trophies aren't the real reason they compete. For the vast majority of esports competitors, esports are a way to chase the dream of being recognized as one of the greatest players in the world!

DID YOU KNOW?

Dota 2 player Kuro Takhasomi has earned over $4.2 million dollars in prize money, making him one of the top-earning esports players ever!

WHERE TO PLAY

PERSONAL COMPUTERS
PCs were first to support online play, so they're very important to the history of esports. Early hits on PC included FPS and strategy titles, leading to MOBAs and battle royale later on!

ARCADES
Social gaming venues like arcades naturally lend themselves to competitive gaming. Many top esports games began in the darkness of the arcade!

CONSOLES
Consoles are the natural home of sports games like *FIFA 19* or fighting games like *Super Smash Bros.*!

MOBILE
Esports on mobile are growing fast, with games like *Vainglory* and *Clash Royale* leading the charge. Smartphone gaming is everywhere!

VIRTUAL REALITY
It's in the early days of this new form of competitive gaming, but VR holds lots of potential for the future!

HOW TO WATCH

Nowadays, there's lots of ways to tune in to competitive gaming. Here are a few of the big ones!

LIVESTREAMING

Websites like Twitch, YouTube, Facebook, and Mixer provide live streams of many major esports events.

VIDEO ON DEMAND

You can find "VODs"—videos of past matches—on many popular video streaming services, particularly YouTube.

LIVE TELEVISION

Depending on where you live, you may find esports on TV! ESPN hosts regular shows in the US.

ESPORTS PORTALS

Certain organizations and game publishers, like Riot Games and Dreamhack, provide esports websites with extra info.

GAMING CONVENTIONS

Major fan conventions like GamesCom and BlizzCon often host esports alongside other gaming action!

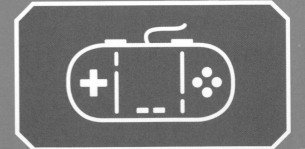

COMPETITIVE EVENTS

Major tournaments—often hosted in huge venues—are the closest you can get to the esports experience!

GLOSSARY

ANALYST
Experts in their field, analysts help explain the action of an esports match to the viewing audience.

BUFF
Making a character or weapon more powerful—this might be temporary, or it might be a permanent change!

CASTER
Short for "broadcaster" or "shoutcaster," a caster commentates on esports action as it happens.

CCG
A collectible card game where players amass a collection of cards and then do battle with custom decks.

FGC
The fighting game community—a close-knit bunch who love all kinds of one-on-one fighting games!

FPS
First-person shooters—games involving gunplay where you perceive the action from your character's perspective.

GG WP
Meaning "good game, well played," these letters are a polite way to let your opponent know you enjoyed the match!

GL HF
Short for "good luck, have fun"—type this at the start of a match to show that you're a good sport who respects your opponent!

META
The metagame is comprised of the strategies that are currently producing the best results for a given game.

MOBA
Multiplayer online battle arenas are games where teams of heroes do battle for gold and resources across a three-lane map.

NERF
When a developer makes a character, weapon, or strategy less effective to balance the game, it's been nerfed.

OBSERVER
Observers are responsible for in-game camera controls, ensuring that viewers don't miss any of the action!

PLAY
In esports, a "play" is a particularly decisive action taken by a player. Top plays are exciting to watch!

PRO
A professional player—somebody who competes in esports events as a full-time job. The dream for many amateurs!

RTS
Real-time strategy—tactical games where battles between armies take place without a break between turns.

SPEEDRUN
The art of completing a singleplayer game as quickly as possible—an esport in its own right!

STRAT
A single strategy. A plan for victory, usually determined by a team captain or coach before the match.

STREAMER
A gamer who livestreams their gameplay to entertain their audience. Many esports pros are streamers, too!

ROCKET LEAGUE

ROCKET-POWERED SOCCER!

KEY INFO
Developer: Psyonix
Publisher: Psyonix
Release date: July 2015
Genre: Sports/Racing
Play it on: PC, PS4, Switch,
Xbox One

BLAST OFF

Rocket League takes soccer to a whole new level by putting players behind the wheels of rocket-powered sports cars as they aim to drive a giant ball into the opposing team's goal. Contained within a glass-walled arena, players can collect boost to drive up and around the walls, or even fly through the air as they battle for control of the ball. There are no set positions, leaving players to jump between the roles of striker, defender, and goalkeeper throughout the match.

With no throw-ins, corners, or offside rules to worry about, Rocket League games are nonstop action as players race back and forth across the arena. Quick reactions, teamwork, and smart ball control spell victory, but it's the flashy aerial shots and saves that really give Rocket League its competitive edge. Think a bicycle kick is impressive? Wait until you see what these cars can do! The very best Rocket League players are masters of a whole new kind of ball game.

DID YOU KNOW?

Rocket League is a sequel to a game with a far less catchy name, Supersonic Acrobatic Rocket-Powered Battle-Cars —SARPBC for short!

⭐ GETTING INTO GEAR

THE GOAL
Hit the ball over the opponent's line to score a goal and cause a flashy explosion.

SPEED BOOST
Use your boost to pick up speed. Go fast enough and you'll turn supersonic, able to destroy enemy cars.

ROCKET BOOST
Drive over these to refill your boost meter. Small packs refill some boost, while big packs fill the whole meter.

WALL DRIVING
You can drive up the walls of the arena to hit the ball or dodge opponents.

JUMP TO IT
Cars can jump once to get airborne, then jump again to flip in a direction and strike the ball.

GETTING AIR
Boosting while airborne will let you fly for a short time. Angle toward the ball for a midair skill shot.

ROCKET LEAGUE CHAMPIONSHIP SERIES

The Rocket League Championship Series (RLCS) is where the best of the best come to compete in 3v3 matches. Each season is split into a North American and European league. Eight skilled teams compete in each league over five weeks, with every side playing the others once. The top six then earn a spot in the Regional Championships where they prove themselves as the best in their class.

Finally, there's the biggest event of all: the World Championships. The four best teams from the North America and Europe RLCS are joined by two from Oceania and South America to duke it out for the ultimate title. Hosted in front of a live audience, the World Championships see Rocket League's six greatest teams fight to square off in a single elimination bracket where just one loss spells disaster. At this point, only the most confident and capable players excel. With so much on the line, each game is an exciting race to claim the trophy and earn the title!

BECOMING A ROCKET STAR
THE LONG ROAD TO THE ROCKET LEAGUE CHAMPIONSHIP SERIES

▶ **OPEN QUALIFIER**
Compete in your region's qualifier without losing two games.

▶ **PLAY-INS**
Face the other qualifying teams in a tournament.

▶ **RIVAL SERIES**
Prove yourself against the top four teams in your region.

TOP TEAMS FROM THE RLCS

European and North American teams dominate the top levels of the RLCS, but the addition of South America in Season 7 and the success of Oceania in Season 6 mean each year brings new surprises—and challengers for the crown!

CLOUD9
This American team upset leaders Dignitas to win the Season 6 World Championships.

RENEGADES
The best of Australia and New Zealand, Renegades have shown that Oceania is no joke.

RENAULT VITALITY
Season 7 champions and winners of the European finals, Vitality excel in one-on-one situations.

LOWKEY ESPORTS
South America is new to global Rocket League, but Lowkey Esports are eager to make an impact.

NRG ESPORTS
NRG are consistent performers who have won the last two North American Finals.

PSG ESPORTS
PSG's long-running roster has been in the game a long time, giving them a great deal of experience.

GROUND ZERO GAMING
This Aussie team (formerly Out of Order) also qualified for the Season 7 finals.

DIGNITAS
Winners of Season 5, storied esports org Dignitas fell just short of victory in Season 6.

FC BARCELONA
Two skilled Brits and a Frenchman form the core of this Spanish-sponsored RLCS team.

ROGUE
A team of wildcards, Rogue's roster includes one of the RLCS' biggest names, Kronovi.

RLCS
Make a name for yourself in the Rival Series and you could score a place in the RLCS.

★ STAR PLAYERS ★

CAMERON "KRONOVI" BILLS
Possibly the first and most famous Rocket League star, Kronovi recently left G2 and joined Rogue.

MARIANO "SQUISHYMUFFINZ" ARRUDA
Canadian SquishyMuffinz is famous for an impressive shot from the ceiling.

MAURICE "YUKEO" WEIHS
Dignitas's Yukeo is one of the only professional players to compete using a mouse and keyboard.

FRANCESCO "KUXIR97" CINQUEMANI
Italian Kuxir has been playing (and winning) Rocket League since the first season of RLCS.

THE SKILLS to PRACTICE

It takes time and effort to master the skills you'll need to play *Rocket League* at the top level.

BACK POST ROTATION

Teammate already in the goal? Head to the far post. From here you can see a lot and block higher shots.

WAIT BEHIND THE LINE

The default position for close saves. Starting from behind the line gives you time to adjust position and cover a wide range of shots.

DEFEND THE BACKBOARD

If your opponents keep bouncing the ball off the backboard, try driving up there in anticipation.

MOVE ON UP

Once the ball has been cleared, don't be afraid to move up to midfield. Be ready to swap places with attacking teammates if they need fuel.

GLOSSARY

50/50
When two players hit the ball at the same time.

ROTATION
When players on the same team change positions to switch up the strategy.

REDIRECT
Changing the direction of the ball midair to trick a defender.

DUNK
Blocking an opponent's hit at very close range and sending it back over them.

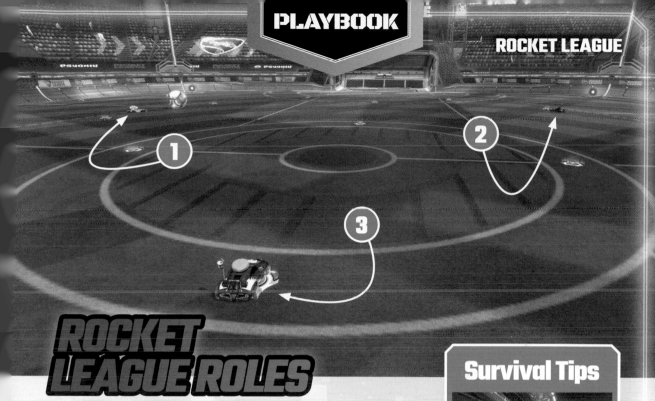

ROCKET LEAGUE ROLES

Unlike a regular soccer match, you'll need to swap between several roles over the course of a *Rocket League* game. That means you'll not only be an attacker, but a support player and goalkeeper, too! The biggest mistakes in *Rocket League* are when teams accidentally put two players in the same spot, leaving a gap in their defense. You could spend all game in goal to work on your saves, but if you want to rival, the best then you'll need to master every place on the pitch. Which role you play will depend on your position, your fuel, and how well you're communicating with your team. Practice with the same side enough and you'll be able to shift between roles effortlessly.

1 CONTESTER
Chase the ball, push it up one side of the field, and attempt to cross or pass to the Striker so they can score.

2 STRIKER
Wait on the opposite side for the Contester to cross or pass, then move in for a rapid finish. Aim true!

3 DEFENDER
Hang back to defend against long shots. Swap positions with players who need to refuel.

Survival Tips

SAVE YOUR FUEL
Front flips can generate speed, letting you save your boost.

WATCH YOUR TEAM
Be aware of your teammates' positions to avoid overlapping.

DRESS TO IMPRESS
Because no car is complete without a ridiculous hat.

KEY INFO
Developer: EA
Publisher: EA
Release date: September 2018
Genre: Sport
Play it on: PS4, Xbox One, Nintendo
Switch, PS3, Xbox 360, PC

FIFA 19

A COMPETITIVE SOCCER PHENOMENON!

BE A SOCCER STAR

One of the world's most popular games, FIFA provides soccer fans with a whole load of different ways to enjoy their favorite sport. There's The Journey, a singleplayer narrative adventure that lets you experience the life of a pro player. There's also career mode that lets you tell your own story as you rise to the top of the game.

For most FIFA players, however, it's all about competition—on the couch or online. *FIFA 19* lets you form a club with other players, climb the ranks of online play, and even participate in tournaments.

The very best FIFA players are able to take everything they know about the game in real life and apply it to the digital field, mastering techniques and strategies that allow them to run rings around their opponents.

Amazing animation and lifelike visuals create an atmospheric rendition of the sport, and *FIFA 19*'s attention to detail means that interactions between players are particularly believable. This is an ideal and endlessly rewarding way to experience the world's favorite sport.

DID YOU KNOW?

EA's FIFA series of games are officially licensed by the world governing body of soccer, providing many exclusive benefits!

PRO TECHNIQUES

ACTIVE TOUCH
This new system allows for greater finesse and more nuanced ball control.

GAME PLANS
Preparation is key. You can customize your tactics to suit your squad ahead of time . . .

DYNAMIC TACTICS
. . . then use the D-pad to change your team's tactics to suit the situation in the match itself.

DUELS
Using the left trigger on your pad can help you protect a contested ball.

TIMED FINISH
An extra button tap can enhance your shot, but be sure to time it right!

TAKING CORNERS
Coordinate your crosser and central striker to score from a corner!

FIFA 20

FIFA 20 continues where FIFA 19 left off, with a new mode—Volta Football—providing more ways to play! The next season of the FIFA eWorld Cup will take place on this new version.

FIFA ESPORTS

FIFA 19 enjoys a thriving esports scene that mirrors the international popularity of traditional soccer. Both EA Games and FIFA themselves run regular events and championships, and many traditional soccer teams now have their own professional esports players too! Competitive matches are played one-on-one, with both players controlling a whole team by themselves.

The road to the Fifa eWorld Cup begins at home—players take part in online tournaments and climb the rankings in order to qualify for the big event. Winners take home hundreds of thousands of dollars in prize money and are given the opportunity to attend special FIFA events and meet some of their favorite soccer celebrities.

You'll find all of the biggest *FIFA 19* events on both Twitch and YouTube, and several finals have even been broadcast on television! FIFA esports provide a way for soccer-loving gamers to show off their talents in front of an audience that includes true luminaries of the game.

THE BIG EVENTS

MILESTONES IN THE FIFA COMPETITIVE CALENDAR

▶ **WEEKEND LEAGUE**
Play online Weekend League matches to become a verified FUT Champion.

▶ **QUALIFICATION COMPETITIONS**
Compete against other top players to earn a spot at a live event.

▶ **GLOBAL SERIES**
Earn Global Series points through events and regular victories online.

TOP PLAYERS

FIFA esports are open to anybody, but only the most talented players are able to rise to the top of the scene every year. Here are a few of the names that rule the game—online and at major events.

MSDOSSARY

With many top titles to his name, Saudi Arabian star player MsDossary is one of the most formidable players in FIFA. He plays for esports organization Team Rogue.

MARCUS GOMES

Marcus Gomes represents Melbourne City FC and has secured solid results both internationally and in his homeland of Australia.

F2TEKKZ

This rising superstar has claimed trophy after trophy. Despite arriving on the scene out of the blue, he now represents both Liverpool FC and England!

JOKSAN

Part of US-based esports organization compLexity Gaming, Joksan delivered great results for his team and country in 2019. He's proof that US soccer is the real deal!

FAZE TASS

As part of the multi-game FaZe esports organization, Tass is known for his consistently strong performances. He also plays for London's Arsenal football club.

TUGA

Portugal's Tuga is known for his defensive play, which has seen him rise to the very top of competitive FIFA and secured him a number of top prizes!

 PLAYOFF QUALIFICATION
Finish in the top 60 to earn a spot at the playoffs.

WORLD CUP GRAND FINAL
The top 16 players progress to the final showdown!

KEY INFO
Developer: EA
Publisher: EA
Release date: August 2018
Genre: Sport
Play it on: PS4, Xbox One, PC

MADDEN NFL 19

BECOME A FOOTBALL STAR!

MAKE YOUR PLAY

EA's *Madden NFL* series is a staple of competitive gaming in the USA: a football simulation with enough depth and detail to satisfy even the most dedicated fans. It's no surprise that a competitive scene has risen up around the game, with the best competitors in the world facing off in the Madden Championship Series in order to earn their place in the biggest event of the season each year —the Madden Bowl.

It's becoming a major part of EA's esports calendar, particularly now that events can be broadcast from the publisher's state-of-the-art esports studio. More and more NFL celebrities are getting involved in Madden esports every year, bringing the game—and its players—even closer to the sport that inspired it!

It takes hard work, careful study, and a strategic mind to become a great competitive Madden player. When the time is right, players over the age of 16 can qualify for the majors by testing their skills against others in online ranked play.

MADDEN NFL 20

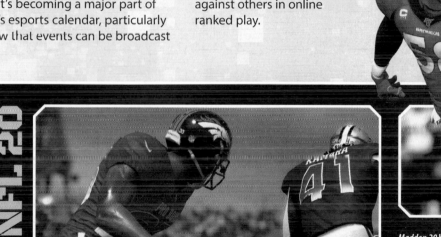

Madden 20 brings some exciting changes to the series' formula, including Superstar X-Factor abilities that set star players in a league of their own—when they're in the zone, there's no stopping them! Also, the addition of run-pass options introduces a highly anticipated play-type and lets the game keep up with the latest developments in the NFL. Seasonal updates like these ensure that Madden players—like their real-life counterparts—must pay close attention to the developing art of the game.

UP YOUR GAME

1

GET FAMILIAR WITH THE BASICS

Madden is a complex simulation of a deep and strategic sport. As a result, it's a great way to learn all of the different considerations that go into every play. However, if you're new to football, then it's worth taking the time to read up on key words and concepts. Do you know what a blitz is? How about a screen pass? If the answer is yes, you're off to a great start—but if not, there are plenty of online resources to help!

2

CHANGE UP YOUR ROUTES

Using the hot routes interface, you can change up your players' running routes on the fly. Maximize your flexibility!

SPIN TO WIN

Offensive players can gain an advantage by using the steerable spin move to evade defenders during a run.

3

4

STUDY PLAYBOOKS

There are a huge number of playbooks in *Madden* and there's lots to be learned by becoming familiar with all of them.

5

REMEMBER TO CELEBRATE

After a big play, you've earned a celebration. Just press both triggers and either A (on Xbox) or X (on PS4) after a touchdown! You can also use this input on the field for a random taunt.

STATS

$700,000	130	37
CLUB CHAMPIONSHIP PRIZE POOL	MILLION COPIES SOLD	MADDEN NFL GAMES

FRANCHISE MODE
Become a better manager!

[C] PAT **SHURMUR**

WR #13
ODELL
BECKHAM JR

LB **OVERVIEW** RB   RATINGS   PROGRESSION HISTORY

95 OVR

OVERALL RATING
Overall Rating——or "OVR"——provides a quick way to see how potent a player is when compared to others.

GOALS

VIEW IN DEPTH CHART

STATS & CONTRACTS

SET AS CAPTAIN

ADD TO TRADE BLOCK

TRADE AWAY

PLAYER PROFILE

HEIGHT:	5'11"
WEIGHT:	198 lb
AGE:	25
EXP:	4 yr
COLLEGE:	LSU

PLAYER ARCHETYPE
In *Madden*, different positions are assessed based on different styles of play. You can see here that Odell Beckham, Jr., a wide receiver, has the "deep threat" archetype.

This player earns XP at the highest rate

PLAYER ARCHETYPES

DEEP THREAT	POSSESSION	RED ZONE THREAT	SLOT
95 OVR	**93** OVR	**93** OVR	**93** OVR

STATS
Madden players are comprised of many different stats, which taken together define their strengths and weaknesses in a match.

SEASON	WEEK 1	WEEK 2	WEEK 3	WEEK 4	WEEK 5
-6	4:25 PM	8:20 PM	4:25 PM	1:00 PM	8:20 PM

[C] JASON **GARRETT**
COACH LEVEL 5 - 150 XP

THINGS TO DO   LB **TEAM** RB   MANAGE   LEAGUE   OPTIONS

SCHEME FIT
This number shows how well your selected scheme fits your current roster of players.

82 OVR   **53/53** PLAYERS

RS **OFFENSE** 87

DEFENSE 81

SPECIAL TEAMS

SPECIALIST

NEW   PRACTICE

MY TEAM

FREE AGENTS

T.SMITH 95	C.WILLIAMS 77	T.FREDERICK 95	Z.MARTIN 96	L.COLLINS 72		G.SWAIM 73
C.GREEN 63	M.MARTIN 69	J.LOONEY 65	J.LOONEY 71	C.FLEMING 68		B.JARWIN 69
C.FLEMING 68	J.LOONEY 71	Z.MARTIN 98		C.GREEN 63		D.SCHULTZ 69
LT A+	LG C+	C	RG	RT C		TE C

VERTICAL ZONE RUN

88% SCHEME FIT

MY COACH

TRADE CENTER

TEAM OVERVIEW
Here you can see an overview of your players' OVRs as well as the defensive and offensive strengths of your team as a whole.

C.BEASLEY 81	E.ELLIOTT 92	D.PRESCOTT 82			A.HURNS 80
T.WILLIAMS 79	R.SMITH 71	M.WHITE 64			D.THOMPSON 77
M.GALLUP 73	B.SCARBROUGH 67	C.RUSH 63			C.WILSON 71
	J.OLAWALE 67				
WR1 B	HB A	QB B	FB C		WR2 B-

HOLD A REORDER

KEY INFO

Developer: Visual Concepts
Publisher: 2K Sports
Release date: September 2018
Genre: Sport
Play it on: PC, Nintendo Switch, PlayStation 4, Xbox One, Android, iOS

NBA 2K19

THE ULTIMATE BASKETBALL SIM!

PLAY LIKE A CHAMP

NBA 2K19 isn't just a sports game—it's a tribute to basketball that gives players the opportunity to not just master the game, but soak in the atmosphere of the court. This can be a tough game to conquer, but the rewards are worth it: Not only does it let you develop your basketball skills across multiple singleplayer and multiplayer modes, but there's a thriving esports scene, too. The very best players get to take their passion for basketball, hone it in *NBA 2K19*, and then take their talents on the road to win fans of their own.

Even if you never take to the big leagues, *NBA 2K19* gives you everything you need to rise to the top on your own terms. MyLeague mode lets you take control of the team of your choice and lead them to victory, while MyCareer mode tells the engaging story of the journey of a young player with dreams of going pro. However you choose to play, *NBA 2K19*'s commitment to the spectacle of basketball shines through.

DID YOU KNOW?

The first *NBA 2K* game came out in 1999 for the Sega Dreamcast console. There have been 24 games since then!

⭐ GET STARTED

PASS AND DRIBBLE
Make sure you use both passing and dribbling to move the ball up the court. Don't be predictable!

CONTEST SHOTS
Get close to opposing players and contest their shots by flicking the right stick upwards.

TAKEOVERS
Pull off passes and clean shots to fill up the takeover meter, which lets you temporarily boost your stats!

WATCH FOR OPENINGS
Whether on offense or defense, you need to look out for open dribbling lanes and shot opportunities.

PREPARE YOUR SHOT
A successful shot needs good positioning, distance from defenders, and good timing. Try to balance each of these.

GREEN MEANS GO!
When the shot bar flashes green, all that prep has paid off and it's time to take your shot!

NBA 2K20

NBA 2K20 is set to deliver new features and improvements that'll ensure that it plays a vital role in the future of the NBA 2K League.

NBA 2K LEAGUE

NBA 2K's esports scene all centers around the *NBA 2K* League, which is run by 2K Games and the NBA itself. It runs in seasons, which begin in the spring and carry on until the finals in the summer. You can catch regular weekly games from Wednesday to Friday, livestreamed on both Twitch and YouTube. These games take place live at the *NBA 2K* League Studio in New York!

Just like in traditional basketball, players become pros by getting chosen by big teams in the annual draft. Before they can get to that point, however, they need to qualify. This means proving their skill by winning more than 100 games in *NBA 2K19*'s Pro-Am mode while winning more than 50% of their matches. It's a tough bar to hit!

There's always new talent coming into the *NBA 2K* League, however, with dozens of new players joining established veterans to play for glory in each new season. The success of the league has seen *NBA 2K19* become a popular crossover between traditional sport and esports.

SEASON SCHEDULE
HOW EACH YEAR IN THE NBA 2K LEAGUE PLAYS OUT.

▶ **REGULAR SEASON**
Teams play for points and position in weekly matches in New York.

▶ **TOURNAMENTS**
Three tournaments every season offer big prize pools and act as important tiebreakers.

▶ **PLAYOFFS**
The best teams go head-to-head at the end of the season with the goal of making it to the finals.

NBA 2K LEAGUE THE TOP TEAMS

The thriving *NBA 2K* League has hundreds of amazing players and teams from all around the USA. Here's ten of the top performers from the 2019 season to get your viewing journey off to a great start.

BLAZER5 GAMING
This formidable team put on a great show in the 2019 season!

MAVS GAMING
An impressive run saw this Dallas-based team reach the 2019 playoffs.

KINGS GUARD
Affiliated with the Sacramento Kings, the Kings Guard are a powerhouse outfit.

PACERS GAMING
The Pacers have turned in good results at several *NBA 2K* League tournaments.

MAGIC GAMING
Top-tier competitors Magic Gaming are affiliated with the Orlando Magic.

76ERS GAMING
The 76ers won The Tipoff, a league tournament in both 2018 and 2019!

CLTX GAMING
This Boston Celtics affiliate were major contenders in the 2019 season.

NETS GC
Top performers with their own training facility in Brooklyn's Barclays Center.

T-WOLVES GAMING
The Minnesota Timberwolves launched their affiliate team for the 2019 season.

CAVS LEGION
These Cleveland Cavaliers affiliates proudly declare that they're like no other team.

▶ **FINALS**
It all comes down to this! After a showdown between the best two teams, a champion is crowned.

★ PRO PLAYERS ★

CHIQUITAE126
Drafted by Warriors Gaming in 2019, Chiquitae126 is the first woman to be drafted into the *NBA 2K* Pro League.

OFAB
This versatile player produced some impressive results in the 2019 season as part of Celtics Crossover Gaming.

RADIANT
This talented point guard has lead his team, the 76ers, to victory after victory in the *NBA 2K* League.

ONEWILDWALNUT
Blazer5's OneWildWalnut is a top-performing player who also plays traditional basketball for his college.

KEY INFO

Developer: Epic Games
Publisher: Epic Games
Release date: July 2017
Genre: Battle Royale
Play it on: PC, PS4, Xbox One,
Switch, iOS, Android

FORTNITE

BATTLE ROYALE BUILDING BONANZA!

WELCOME TO THE ISLAND

When *Fortnite* released in July 2017, it was a very different game to the worldwide phenomenon it has become. *Save The World* was the only version of *Fortnite* at launch—the co-op wave-based survival mode was all the game was meant to be, but Epic developed the mode we all know and love in under two months for a September release.

Since then, the 100 player battle royale has exploded in popularity, with over 250 million registered players around the world, including some celebrities like rapper Drake and soccer player Mesut Ozil. It's safe to say *Fortnite* is one of the most influential titles of this generation of games.

One hundred players dive down from the battle bus that flies over the map, and have to search for weapons and loot to help them build and survive. The playable area shrinks as a storm encroaches on the island, pushing players closer together until only two players remain for a thrilling final duel.

DID YOU KNOW?

The island is always evolving as locations are replaced over time —like Flush Factory, a toilet factory that used to be where Happy Hamlet is now!

⭐ WEAPON TYPES

ASSAULT RIFLES
Best for mid- or long-range combat and a staple in any serious player's inventory.

SUBMACHINE GUNS
Great at spraying down walls and enemies alike, but only when you're up close and personal!

SHOTGUNS
Another must-have, shotguns are perfect for dealing a lot of damage at close range.

SNIPER RIFLES
Spotted someone too far to shoot with an assault rifle? Whip out a sniper rifle!

EXPLOSIVES
Destroy someone's buildings or spam explosives at enemies for serious damage.

PISTOLS
They may not pack the heaviest punch, but pistols can be useful in a pinch!

FORTNITE WORLD CUP

Fortnite's esports scene is still getting started, but that hasn't stopped Epic from providing the big bucks. The 2019 finals took place in New York City from July 26–28 and players competed for their share of $30 million, on top of the millions that were up for grabs during the qualification process.

Qualifiers lasted for 10 weeks, alternating between solos and duos. Absolutely anybody could compete in the open tournaments to try and progress through to the finals—most esports are limited to established pro players who have the backing of an organization, but since the *Fortnite* World Cup is open to anybody, it was the perfect time for unproven players to make a breakthrough.

This was the first ever World Cup, and at the rate *Fortnite* is growing, the players who made a name for themselves in New York were laying the foundation for a long, successful career as the best *Fortnite* players in the world. Not bad for a game less than two years old, eh?

OFFICIAL *FORTNITE* TOURNAMENTS
EVERY EPIC-SANCTIONED *FORTNITE* EVENT

▶ **SUMMER SKIRMISH**
Summer 2018 spanned 8 weeks for $8 million total.

▶ **FALL SKIRMISH**
$10 million was up for grabs in the next six-week tournament.

▶ **IN-GAME TOURNAMENTS**
In-game tournaments were added in October 2018.

TOP *FORTNITE* PLAYERS

Here are some of the best *Fortnite* players in the world—players who made their mark at the World Cup and who promise to make a big splash in the future, too!

TFUE
Tfue is one of the world's best and is currently without a team after leaving FaZe Clan. That won't stay the case for long!

GHOST AYDAN
Despite the World Cup being played on PC, Aydan is one of the only players to insist on using a controller.

SOLARY KINSTAAR
Kinstaar killed Ninja in the duos warm-up match at the 2018 *Fortnite* Pro-Am!

ATLANTIS MITRO
Mitr0 is known as one of the very best in Europe, teaming with Mongraal in duos.

SECRET MONGRAAL
Mongraal is just 14 years old, making him one of the youngest people to compete at the World Cup.

NATE HILL
Nate was once disqualified from the Fall Skirmish, but he returned with a vengeance to take on all comers at the World Cup.

SLAYA
Slaya was the very first person to qualify for the World Cup, since he placed first in week one.

RONALDO
Sharing a name with one of the world's greatest soccer players, Ronaldo is definitely one to watch.

LENAIN
LeNain was the only player from Team EnVy to make it to the World Cup—that's a lot of pressure to succeed!

CLOAK
FaZe Cloak missed out on qualifying for the World Cup, even though his long-time duo buddy Tfue made it through.

WORLD CUP QUALIFIERS
10 weeks of qualifiers started in April 2019.

FORTNITE WORLD CUP
The World Cup took place in New York in July 2019.

NOTABLE SEASONS

SEASON 4
The meteor crashed into Dusty Divot and craters were spread throughout the map, causing chaos and carnage.

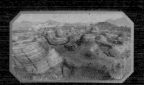

SEASON 5
Moisty Mire was replaced by an entire desert, including Paradise Palms, while Anarchy Acres was turned into a golf course called Lazy Links.

SEASON 7
The Ice King crashed his iceberg into the island and the southwest corner became shrouded in snow.

SEASON 8
A volcano appeared and erupted over Wailing Woods, which was later turned into the Pressure Plant.

EARLY GAME PREP

PLAN OF ACTION

Every game of *Fortnite* is different, depending on where the safe zone ends up, but you need to have a rough plan of action in your head from the get-go. Where are you going to land, what weapons do you want to find, and where are you going to run to afterward? Having a plan means you can optimize your game, rather than dwelling on decisions mid-game!

FARM MATERIALS

Building is just as important as weaponry, so make sure you're stocked up by destroying trees and rocks!

PICK YOUR DESTINATION

Land near the edge of the map for some peace, or go centrally to fight players from the start!

RUN TO SAFETY

If you're not in the safe zone, flee from the storm and stick to the edge of the circle to avoid other players!

BUILD SHELTER

If you don't have natural cover, make sure you take shelter by building a small base or tower!

STATS

99 OTHER PLAYERS TO BEAT

5 ITEMS IN YOUR INVENTORY

999 OF EACH MATERIAL TYPE

BUILDING BASICS

STAIRS
Stairs are your best friend when building, because no incline is insurmountable whether you're climbing a mountain or in a fight.

WALL
Walls can defend you from all angles and even though they'll be shot down a lot, just build another!

FLOOR
They can help you descend mountains, bridge gaps to enemy structures, and place traps for unsuspecting foes!

ROOF
The least used building piece, roofs are excellent for protecting your floors from gunshots underneath, and allowing you to peek out of windows.

FAMOUS SKINS

A whistle-stop tour of some of *Fortnite*'s most famous skins.

ROYALE BOMBER

The Royale Bomber skin is exclusively available with PS4 console or controller purchases, so if you find one of these heroic skins, the player is truly dedicated to the game.

BLACK KNIGHT

The final battle pass skin for Season 2, if you see a Black Knight in the wild, you know you're up against a veteran *Fortnite* player and you'll have a tough fight on your hands.

SUPER STRIKER

There's a number of soccer player variations but it's got a reputation for being a skin used by highly skilled players, so be on your guard because they're more than capable of scoring some goals.

THE REAPER

Known as "John Wick" before the official John Wick skin was released, The Reaper was available at Tier 100 in Season 3 and was super popular due to how incredibly cool he looks.

GLOSSARY

CAMPING
Hiding in one place for too long and not searching for enemies.

ONE SHOT
When an enemy is so low they'll die in one shot.

ROTATE
Moving into the next safe zone, especially in the late game.

SHIELDS
A second health bar which can hold an extra 100 health.

FISHSTICK

Fishstick is the ultimate meme skin; with his wavy arms, nonplussed expression, and huge eyes, every emote looks hilarious . . . especially Breezy!

PLACES OF INTEREST

The *Fortnite* map has plenty of locations to investigate across four different biomes, from the snowy southwest to the jungle in the northeast and the desert in the southeast. Every place of interest provides unique terrain, and while great loot can be found all over the map, understanding the lay of the land is crucial if you want to survive till the end of the match. Here's four key locations on the island, each offering different opportunities to players who land there.

1 NEO TILTED

Usually the busiest location on the entire map, Neo Tilted is a futuristic city and it's the place to land if you want nonstop action!

2 PARADISE PALMS

The biggest city in the desert, Paradise Palms has a huge hotel full of loot, which provides a great scouting spot to look over the entire town.

3 HAPPY HAMLET

A quaint village, Happy Hamlet is found on the south coast and has a lot of loot! It's usually pretty quiet, too, so you can take your time looting.

4 DUSTY DIVOT

Dusty Divot is a great place to farm wood, and when you've looted the middle, make sure you loot the diner on the north side.

Single Use Items

HEALING
Use these essential items to restore health or shields after a fight.

GRENADES
From Frag to Impulse, grenades can be used in a variety of ways.

TRAPS
Anything you can attach to a floor or wall is a trap.

BUGHA

KEY FACTS

Name: Kyle "Bugha" Giersdorf
Origin: United States of America
Company: Sentinels
Games played: *Fortnite*
Playing since: 2019

Bugha burst onto the Fortnite esports scene with a massive 1st place finish at the first ever Fortnite World Cup. Going from a relative unknown to a superstar in just a few months, Bugha began his professional career when he took part in a fairly minor Blackheart Cup online tournament. Though he placed low, he proceeded to enter the 2019 World Cup Qualifier and eventually earned himself one of 100 spots in the World Cup Solo Finals. Bugha dominated the competition and went into the final royale as the overwhelming leader in the standings, eventually sealing the deal to become the first ever Fortnite World Champion!

KEEP CALM AND BUILD ON:

Thanks to Bugha's next level building skills he was able to constantly stay one step ahead— and above—his competition. When in doubt, build higher!

PATIENCE, PATIENCE, PATIENCE:

While some players favor a more aggressive style, Bugha tends to let play a bit more passively, mostly letting his opponents come to him. Defense wins games!

PRACTICE MAKES PERFECT:

According to Bugha, it takes plenty of practice in order to compete on the highest level—at least six hours a day. "I've just dedicated all of my time to improving and getting better."

TOP OF HIS GAME

So what do you do after winning one of the biggest esports championships of all time? You go back to school. Bugha was only 16 years old when he clinched the #1 spot at the Fortnite World Cup and earned $3,000,000 in prize money. He's not done competing, though, not by a long shot! Just a few weeks after his massive solo win, Bugha got right back to business, entering multiple *Fortnite* team tournaments and achieving multiple top 8 finishes. Bugha's drive to win is massive—it's no surprise that he's at the top of the Fortnite eSports world!

MAJOR VICTORIES

▶ 2019 FORTNITE WORLD CUP
▶ TRIO CASH CUP 2 - NAE

FORTNITE ARENA MODE DIVISIONS:

Open I: 0 to 499 Hype

Open II: 500 to 999 Hype

Open III: 1,000 to 1,499 Hype

Open IV: 1,500 to 1,999 Hype

Contender I: 2,000 to 2,999 Hype

Contender II: 3,000 to 4,499 Hype

Contender III: 4,500 to 6,499 Hype

Champion I: 6,500 to 9,999 Hype

Champion II: 10,000 to 13,999 Hype

Champion III: 14,000+ Hype

APEX LEGENDS

A LEGENDARY BATTLE ROYALE!

KEY INFO

Developer: Respawn Entertainment
Publisher: Electronic Arts
Release date: February 2019
Genre: FPS
Play it on: PC, PS4, Xbox One

FIGHT FOR GLORY!

Apex Legends is a 60-person battle royale where teams of three players plummet into a massive arena. Only one team can win at the end of the match, and the arena is constantly shrinking. Each team is made up of "legends"—characters who have powerful abilities. Will you pick Lifeline, the supportive healer who throws out healing drones and summons care packages for her team? How about a high-damage character like Wraith, who can vanish into the void and summon portals?

Each character can make use of the many different weapons you'll find across the map, and has the ability to jump, climb, and slide. With nearly limitless mobility, you've got lots of opportunities to set up ambushes, outplay your opponents, and claim the title of legend for yourself!

Building a squad with the right combination of legends, working with your team, and mastering the art of skirmishing and gunplay is essential to winning in this high-pressure game. Luckily, there's a legend for everyone, and it's easy to get into the action.

⭐ YOUR LEGEND

BANGALORE: PROFESSIONAL SOLDIER
Bangalore relies on speed, her smoke launcher, and sheer firepower to take out her enemies.

BLOODHOUND: TECHNOLOGICAL TRACKER
Bloodhound follows the old ways, using high-powered scanners to track their foes.

MIRAGE: HOLOGRAPHIC TRICKSTER
Bamboozled! Mirage's holographic clones sow chaos on the battlefield. Make sure you're aiming at the right Mirage!

CAUSTIC: TOXIC TRAPPER
Getting close to Caustic is tough thanks to his array of poison mines and powerful gas grenade ultimate. Keep your distance!

OCTANE: ADRENALINE JUNKIE
Octane moves fast and relishes a tough fight. It's hard to take this guy out, especially when he puts down his jump pad!

PATHFINDER: FORWARD SCOUT
Pathfinder's eager to please his team with ziplines, covering fire, and map scouting. Don't underestimate his mobility!

REACH THE APEX

Here's how to pull off legendary maneuvers in the world of Apex Legends.

MASTER YOUR ABILITIES ▷

Mirage's Decoy or Wraith's Dimensional Rift take time and effort to perfect. Play these characters until you nail the timing and nuance of their abilities. You'll fail a lot before you master them!

WATCH YOUR SURROUNDINGS ▷

It can be hard to spot enemies, and against stealthy or mobile foes it can be easy to find yourself in an ambush. Move slowly and always keep an eye out!

CHECK YOUR WEAPONS ▷

Make sure you're using weapons that suit your playstyle! Every Legend needs to rely on weapons, no matter their abilities, and shotguns, sniper rifles, and pistols each have distinct strengths and weaknesses.

GLOSSARY

BANNERS
Items that give you a chance to call defeated teammates back to the battle!

PING
An on-screen notification from an ally. Apex's system is very versatile—use it!

JUMP TOWER
These launch points let you return to the sky to redeploy somewhere else.

ATTACHMENTS
Upgrades like scopes and larger magazines that improve your gear.

WORK WITH YOUR TEAM! ▷

Make sure you're always staying near your allies, especially if you're playing as a character like Lifeline. Running off on your own puts your teammates at risk!

APEX LEGENDS

RUNOFF

BUNKER

AIRBASE

BRIDGES

SWAMPS

2

HYDRO DAM

MARKET

1

SKULL TOWN

REPULSOR

3

THUNDERDOME

WATER TREATMENT

KNOW THE LAND

 If you want to come out on top in *Apex Legends*, you have to understand the map. At the start of every match, a jumpship arcs its away across the arena, and your squad's jumpmaster will choose when to drop and where to land. Because the dropship heads in a different direction each time, there's no one perfect spot to land. Instead, you'll want to choose a place that has lots of buildings or loot, and preferably as few enemy squads as possible. Make sure you watch for the brightly colored plumes of smoke that come from other squads as they drop! High-loot areas can be the most valuable and get your squad ready the fastest, but they're also the most contested. Be careful and try lots of locations on the map to find your favorite spot to drop.

Weapons Of Choice

PEACEKEEPER
This shotgun is extremely powerful and rewards skillful play

WINGMAN
A steady aim will help you get the most out of this potent pistol.

SPITFIRE
Lots of ammo and controllable recoil makes this machine gun a surefire hit.

1

THUNDERDOME

A high-risk, high-reward landing spot. A fight will almost always break out here!

2

THE SWAMPS

There are a lot of small buildings here separated by narrow walkways. Tread carefully.

3

SUPPLY SHIP

The supply ship moves across the map. Board it when it lands, or try to drop on top!

KEY INFO
Developer: Bluehole, PUBG Corp
Publisher: PUBG Corp
Release date: March 2017
Genre: Battle Royale
Play it on: PC, XB1, PS4, Mobile

PLAYERUNKNOWN'S
BATTLEGROUNDS

THE ORIGINAL BATTLE ROYALE!

BATTLE BEGINS

There aren't very many developers who can say that they're responsible for the popularity of an entire genre. One such is Brendan Greene, also known as "PlayerUnknown." Greene got his start making "battle royale" mods for military simulators. He then took this concept and expanded it into *PlayerUnknown's Battlegrounds*, which is now one of the biggest games in the world!

At the start of the game, you are one of a hundred players who are flown across a large area in a plane. You choose where to land and must scavenge for supplies, but beware: Areas with more goodies, like cities and towns, will have more players waiting to eliminate you. As time goes on, the playable area closes, and you must fight for survival. In the end, only one player or group will survive and win the game. Battle royale has become a massive genre in its own right, but *PUBG* is still a smash hit for competitive players. It rewards careful planning, a strategic approach, and good aim with thrilling battles across believable landscapes and sprawling cities.

DID YOU KNOW?

Having trouble holding your stuff? Not only do backpacks help you hold more gear—armor will provide space for goodies as well. Extra bandages, anyone?

⭐ GETTING AROUND PUBG

UAZ
You can cruise around in these popular four-person vehicles with or without a roof.

MOTORCYCLE
These are the fastest vehicles in the game, but if you're not careful, you might flip off!

BUGGY
You and a friend can cover some serious distance in this quick, but hard-to-steer, kart.

PG 117
If you need to get three of your friends through the water, this might be your go-to.

AQUARAIL
Making a daring escape with a friend? Nothing beats a classic, speedy Jet Ski to get you across a river!

CARS
There are lots of different cars to find. They tend to offer a ton of speed on roads, but struggle on rough terrain.

WINNER WINNER

While *PUBG* is an intense battle royale game, have no fear! These tips will have you battling with the best.

EARS UP ▽

Don't ignore the world around you! Footsteps, a car engine, or even a plane may give you clues about what's going on. Stay quiet when entering a new area!

FOLLOW CRATES

Even if you don't get what's in the crate, others may try to grab the loot within. Follow them, spring an ambush, and take their stuff instead!

KEEP MOVING ◁

It's easy to forget that the playable area is always shrinking. Don't ignore the timer or linger too long in one place!

GLOSSARY

GEAR
Armor and helmets—higher levels are more effective.

VAULTING
Jumping over walls, through windows, and onto cars. Parkour action!

PLAY AREA
The safe area marked by a circle on the map. Gets smaller as time goes on.

SHACK
This tiny building can barely fit two people inside.

PRACTICE BRAVELY ▷

Just like any game, the key to doing better is to practice. And sometimes, that means diving into the action. Worst case, you lose and start again!

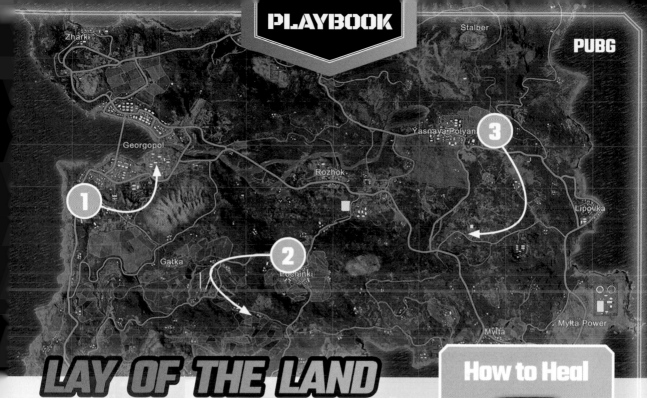

LAY OF THE LAND

The original *PUBG* map, Erangel, has maintained its solid reputation for a reason. With rolling hills, tight forests, sprawling beaches, and plenty of towns and cities, there's a battle environment for everyone. Of course, that also means that once the map's restricted areas start closing in, you might not get to pick your battles in an ideal location. If you were hiding in the grass, you might get pushed toward the beach. If you're a fish in the water, you may need to crawl up a hill on your belly.

Erangel sets the stage for the other three maps in *PUBG*: Miramar, a desert; Vikendi, a snowy setting; and Sanhok, a Southeast Asian island. On the map above, we've indicated examples of places that you'll find on every map, though their details may change. Adapting your approach for each new environment is key—and always be sure to scout a new area from a distance before heading in!

How to Heal

FIRST AID KIT
These large health kits will instantly heal you to 75 health. Share them around!

BANDAGES
You'll find lots of these lying around. Each heals 10 points over time, and can't be used to take you above 75 health.

ENERGY DRINK
Each chug of this adds to your boost bar, which in turn causes you to heal slowly and move more quickly!

CITIES
Filled with tall buildings. Move slowly and listen for footsteps!

TOWNS
Less loot than cities, but it's easier to spot foes before they spot you!

FORTS
These are safe spots until the play area closes in—don't stay!

51

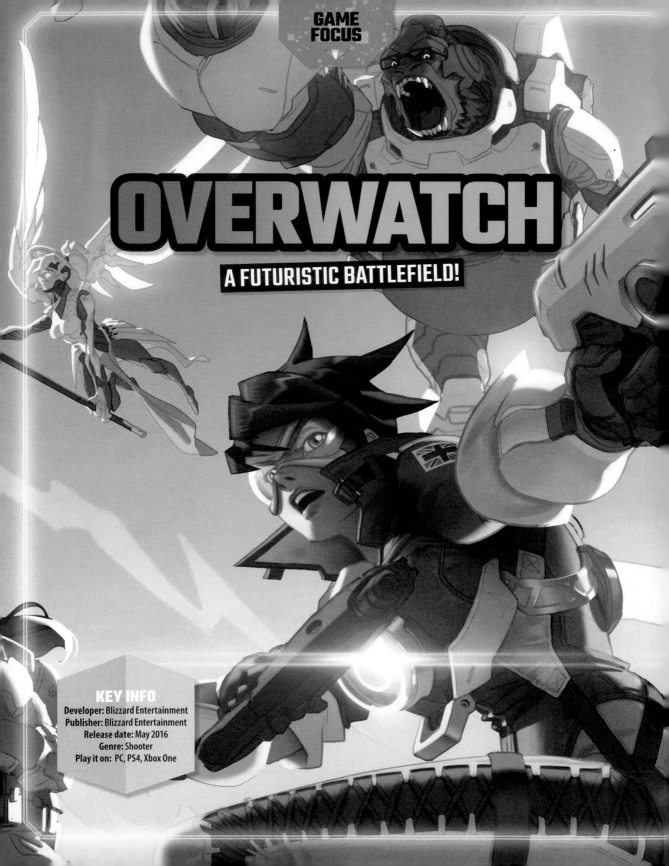

OVERWATCH

A FUTURISTIC BATTLEFIELD!

KEY INFO

Developer: Blizzard Entertainment
Publisher: Blizzard Entertainment
Release date: May 2016
Genre: Shooter
Play it on: PC, PS4, Xbox One

HEROES NEVER DIE...

Blizzard's brilliant shooter pits teams of heroes against one another in a fast-paced battle for supremacy. In *Overwatch*, players have to combine their skills to achieve objectives and overcome the enemy team. It's a great game because it lets players choose a character that suits the way they want to play. Will you wield Tracer's twin blasters and dash into battle, or use Mercy's healing beam to keep your friends in the fight? Teams need players of every kind to work together if they're going to succeed.

Overwatch matches take place on a variety of maps, and each map has a different set of objectives. In Assault mode, one team must capture control points while the other team defends them. In Control, both teams wrestle for control of a single point. In Escort, one team must push a special payload along a track until it reaches the enemy base. A lot of clever strategy goes into winning a game of *Overwatch* —with plenty of exciting action along the way!

DID YOU KNOW?

Blizzard spent many years working on an MMO called *Titan*. It didn't work out, but many of its characters made their way into *Overwatch*.

⭐ HEROIC ABILITIES

D.VA'S SELF-DESTRUCT
D.Va launches her MEKA across the battlefield, where it does massive damage after a short delay.

LÚCIO'S AMP IT UP
Lúcio takes his healing or speed boost aura and boosts its power, amplifying its effects for his allies.

ASHE'S B.O.B.
Ashe summons her robot pal B.O.B. to knock opponents around before letting rip with blasters!

MEI'S ICE WALL
Freeze! Mei creates a barrier in front of her that blocks movement and abilities for both teams.

REINHARDT'S BARRIER FIELD
Reinhardt holds up an energy shield that protects everybody standing behind him.

WRECKING BALL'S ROLL
Wrecking Ball surges forward in ball form, going fast and damaging opponents.

DID YOU KNOW?

The London Spitfire won the Grand Finals over the Philadelphia Fusion to become the 2018 league champions.

OVERWATCH LEAGUE

The Overwatch League is where the best *Overwatch* players connect and compete. Twenty teams from around the world, including China, Korea, France, and the UK, are placed in the Pacific and Atlantic Divisions. Every season is split into four stages, and teams compete each week to earn points and climb the rankings. The best teams head to the Playoffs and Stage Finals, and it all culminates with the Grand Finals to finally establish the best team of the whole season.

Those teams face off in front of crowds both in Los Angeles and abroad. Overwatch League fans show up in full warpaint to support their favorite teams, especially for pivotal matches like the Battle for Los Angeles between the Gladiators and the Valiant, or the Defiant and Titans' Battle for Canada.

Only the best teams can take the trophy, but every team has fans who are rooting for their players to earn glory in the Blizzard Arena!

ROAD TO THE BIG LEAGUES

HOW TO GO FROM AMATEUR TO PRO IN *OVERWATCH*

▶ **OPEN DIVISION**
Play Competitive Play matches in-game until you reach Open Division.

▶ **CONTENDER TRIALS**
Compete against the other top Open Division teams in a tournament.

▶ **OVERWATCH CONTENDERS**
Take part in annual seasons as part of an amateur Contenders team.

THE TEAMS OF THE OVERWATCH LEAGUE

Each team in the Overwatch League has its own branding, style, and roster. No team can win forever, so fans often choose which team to cheer for based on their location, interests, and even favorite colors.

ATLANTA REIGN
Atlanta chose the emblem of the phoenix to represent their tenacity and resilience.

BOSTON UPRISING
The first team to have an undefeated stage, completed in Season 1.

DALLAS FUEL
Formerly Team Envy, the Dallas Fuel are one of the oldest outfits in competitive *Overwatch*.

NEW YORK EXCELSIOR
Considered the strongest team in Season 1, but fell short of the finals.

SEOUL DYNASTY
Seoul of South Korea are hard to beat and can take a win even in the most unexpected situations.

SAN FRANCISCO SHOCK
The Shock fought for the stage one championship in Season 2.

PHILADELPHIA FUSION
The surprise runners-up of Season 1, this is a team that could take the trophy.

TORONTO DEFIANT
From the mean streets of Toronto, the Defiant like to have a lot of attitude with their red and black brand.

VANCOUVER TITANS
One of the most powerful and unstoppable teams in Season 2.

▶ **OVERWATCH LEAGUE**
Rise to the top of your game and you might get scouted for an Overwatch League team.

★ STAR PLAYERS ★

SCOTT "CUSTA" KENNEDY
This friendly Australian played for the Dallas Fuel before leading the Los Angeles Valiant to victory at the Pacific Champions.

PONGPHOP "MICKIE" RATTANASANGCHOD
Mickie is the always smiling face of the Dallas Fuel and proudly represents Thailand in the League.

LANE "SUREFOUR" ROBERTS
Lane is best known for his sniper play and sassy personality.

KIM "GEGURI" SE-YEON
Geguri is the first female player in the League, and she loves both playing tanks and making frog puns.

A TITANIC DEFENSE!

READY TO FIGHT

The Vancouver Titans and San Francisco Shock met in the grand finals of stage one of the Overwatch League's second season. Both teams are running tank-heavy compositions so that they can survive damage and group together for team fights. San Francisco took the first map, and now Vancouver is tasked with defending their payload on the escort map Numbani. Here, the Shock players decide to start with an aggressive approach by taking the high ground before the payload.

RALLY TO ME

The Titans use their support ultimates and group up on the point to eliminate the Shock players and keep their payload safe.

AGGRESSIVE PUSH

San Francisco push onto the point with their tanks leading the way, forcing the Vancouver Titans back into the street.

TANK COMBO

A perfectly placed Graviton Surge from the Titans allows them to group the Shock players up and wipe them out!

DEFENDERS HOLD!

This is a great example of defensive teamwork. By carefully coordinating their counterattack, the Titans are able to turn the game around! Remember this tactic the next time you find yourself on the back foot.

STATS

8,946 BUMPER'S HERO DAMAGE AT 10 MINS

4:26 THE TITANS' FINAL ESCORT TIMER

16.9:4 TWILIGHT'S KILL/DEATH RATIO AT 10 MINS

STUDY YOUR E LAY

Do you want to play like a pro? Studying your own replays is a great way to identify your strengths and weaknesses.

STATE OF PLAY
Pay attention to friendly and enemy health bars. Were you helping the right teammates, or focusing on the most vulnerable foes?

PLAYER'S-EYE VIEW
Viewing a replay in first person helps you understand what your allies and foes could see at crucial moments in the match.

DID YOU KNOW?
Overwatch has a rich backstory. You'll only see a glimpse of it in-game, but check out the official website for comics, short movies, and more!

A DIFFERENT PERSPECTIVE
Changing the camera angle can reveal hidden threats. Bet you didn't spot this Bastion lurking in the corner of the image above!

SIGNS OF BATTLE
Pay attention to where your allies fall—and how. Learning to spot when players have pushed too far helps you avoid mistakes!

BE A TEAM PLAYER

By switching to the right heroes mid game, you can turn a tough match around.

DPS

By dishing out damage, these heroes secure objectives and eliminate priority targets like healers. DPS characters rely on tanks and healers to stay alive and get high damage numbers.

SUPPORT

These heroes have healing abilities that restore their allies and save them from enemies. They'll always need an assist from their tanks, and they damage allies to stay alive and in the fight.

FLEX

Some players switch between damage heroes like Genji and Tracer, and off tanks like Zarya or Roadhog, to provide flexible advantages. Switching takes skill but offers many benefits.

TANK

A tank protects its allies. Whether that's by charging in with power armor, or by jumping in and slamming the ground, tanks want to be in the action.

GLOSSARY

COMP
Composition is the six heroes a team chooses to play.

DIVE
A three tank/three support team aggressive composition.

TAG
A mobile composition based on diving into the enemy's backlines.

MAIN
Taking an objective while the controlling team is elsewhere.

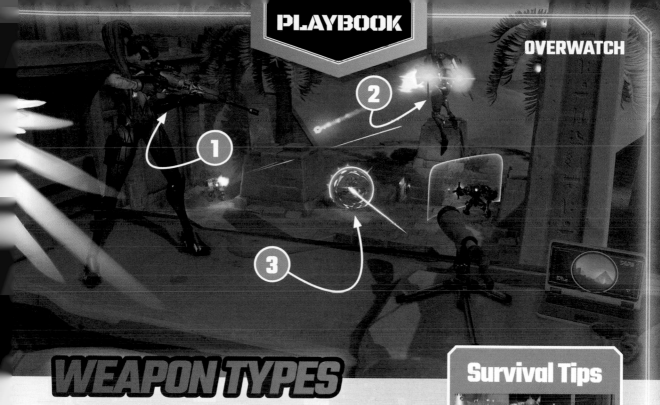

WEAPON TYPES

Understanding how each weapon works allows players to come up with team compositions, combinations, and counters. Hitscan heroes are often seen as more reliable, while projectile heroes need the right conditions to reach their maximum potential. There are lots of ways for heroes to fire, and understanding them can help you figure out why different heroes work in pro play. Understanding enemy weapons will help prevent you and your teammates from taking too much unnecessary damage next time you're contesting a vital point.

① HITSCAN

Weapons like Widowmaker's Widow's Kiss or Tracer's pulse pistols do damage the instant that they're fired. This makes accurate fire hard to dodge.

② PROJECTILE

These weapons have a travel time and can be dodged or countered with hero abilities. Some are explosive, like Pharah's rocket launcher.

③ BEAMS

Beams go straight through certain defenses. Zarya's particle cannon is a hitscan beam while Mei's endothermic blaster is a projectile weapon.

Survival Tips

USE EVERY TOOL
Abilities boost your weapons—don't forget to use them.

THE ULT ECONOMY
Remember that dealing damage charges a hero's ultimate meter more quickly.

BRACE FOR IMPACT
Abilities like Particle Barrier and Defense Matrix can stop offensive skills.

STARCRAFT II

STRATEGY IN SPACE!

KEY INFO
Developer: Blizzard Entertainment
Publisher: Blizzard Entertainment
Release date: July 2010
Genre: Real-Time Strategy
Play it on: PC

FIGHT FOR SUPREMACY

StarCraft II reinvented Blizzard's classic RTS title for a new generation of keyboard warriors. Players choose from one of three iconic races: the versatile Terrans, the overwhelming Zerg, or the spiritual Protoss. Like other RTS games, StarCraft II challenges players to gather resources as fast as possible all while developing their armies and preparing for war. Conflicts over minerals and gas are often the most pivotal moments of a match, as even slight interruptions to one's economy can snowball into a loss.

The best StarCraft II players are experts at scouting and exploiting their opponents' weaknesses at every stage. They're able to disrupt mineral gathering with annoying attacks early on, harass expansion bases during larger fights, and force mistakes through clever positioning with just the right mix of units. This intricate mix of timed attacks and precise unit control makes StarCraft II one of the most challenging games to master, but it's also one of the most satisfying gaming experiences available today.

⭐ LEGENDARY FOES

MARINE
The heart of the Terran army, Marines are reliable troops who can deal with almost any threat both on the ground or in the air.

SIEGE TANK
These huge tanks can transform into long-range artillery cannons that obliterate groups of light ground units and buildings.

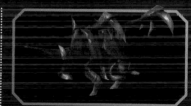

ZERGLING
Cheap and numerous, Zerglings can outmaneuver and surround opponents who aren't careful with their positioning.

QUEEN
Queens defend Zerg hatcheries from early attacks, boost unit production, and can help spread Zerg influence across the map.

ZEALOT
Their high health and shields make Zealots a threat early on, plus hearty meat shields later on in the game.

COLOSSUS
This massive walker can scale cliffs and burn ground units with its lasers, making enemy numbers count for nothing.

STARCRAFT II WORLD CHAMPIONSHIP SERIES

Unlike Overwatch League, Blizzard has stuck to a more traditional framework for the WCS. Though it varies slightly from year to year, the WCS is split between a series of Korean and international tournaments for players of those corresponding regions. For the 2019 season, the WCS offered four circuit events and three "Challenger" qualifying events. There was also one stand-alone tournament at Intel Extreme Masters Katowice, as well as a global All-Star event. Individual players from the international division fought through a series of group stages and playoff brackets for their shot at cash prizes, and WCS points toward a shot at the WCS Global Finals.

The WCS Global Finals featured the top eight players from both divisions. They fought for a piece of a $500,000 prize pot and international bragging rights in front of a live audience and thousands of fans watching from around the world—proof that *StarCraft II*'s long-running esports scene is going strong!

TECH TIMELINE
HOW *STARCRAFT* ARMIES GEAR UP FOR WAR!

▶ **TIER 1**
Basic units that do not require special buildings or research.

▶ **TIER 2**
Units and upgrades that require unique tech or production buildings.

INTERNATIONAL PRO GAMERS

StarCraft II has picked up where its predecessor, *StarCraft: Brood War*, left off in terms of attracting talent from around the world. Unlike team-based esports, each *StarCraft II* pro only has themself to rely on, making every drama-filled match incredible to watch.

▸ JOONA "SERRAL" SOTALA

Serral famously won all Circuit tournaments as Zerg in 2018, and is the only non-Korean player to win a WCS Global Finals in that same year.

▸ KIM "SOS" YOO-JIN

SOS is a legendary StarCraft II player who became the first to be a two-time WCS Global Finals champion in 2015.

▸ LEE "ROGUE" BYUNG-RYUL

This highly unorthodox Zerg player has many first place finishes, including consecutive IEM wins at Shanghai and Katowice.

▸ JUAN CARLOS "SPECIAL" TENA LOPEZ

This highly regarded Terran player from Mexico won every season of the Copa America tournament in 2018—an

▸ TOBIAS "SHOWTIME" SIEBER

Germany's favorite Protoss (an alien species) player has proven himself as one of the best after winning the WCS Spring 2016.

▸ GABRIEL "HEROMARINE" SEGAT

HeRoMaRinE has won multiple Electronic Sports League tournaments and has consistently placed in the top five at WCS events.

▸ ALEX "NEEB" SUNDERHAFT

Neeb was the first foreign player to win a premier *StarCraft II* event in Korea at the 2016 KeSPA Cup—a historic moment!

▸ KIM "CLASSIC" DOH-WOO

Classic was one of SK Telecom T1's best players before they disbanded. He is currently a top player in Korea's Global Starcraft League.

▸ SASHA "SCARLETT" HOSTYN

First to win a *StarCraft* event supported by the Olympic Committee, and the first female player to win a premier SCII event!

▸ KIM "STATS" DAE-YEOB

A veteran of the *StarCraft* community, Stats is a top Korean player and champion of multiple premier events.

▸ TIER 2.5
More expensive and specialized units unlocked within Tier 2.

▸ TIER 3
The highest level units that hit the hardest or offer the most benefits.

63

SCARLETT

KEY FACTS

Name: Sasha "Scarlett" Hoyston
Origin: Canada
Company: Newbee
Games played: Starcraft 2
Playing since: 2011

asha "Scarlett" Hostyn is a prolific *Starcraft 2* pro player who has played in over 180 tournaments and has earned nearly 100 top 4 finishes. A Zerg main, Scarlett is best known for her aggressive, often all-or-nothing style. It's a play-style that she developed and perfected during the years she spent living and training in Korea—the absolute cutting edge region when it comes to *Starcraft 2*. It was there that Scarlett first made a name for herself, becoming one of only three non-native players to win a premier Starcraft tournament in **Korea**. Her skills and determination have made her the most successful female professional gamer of all time!

PRO TIPS

▶ A BOLD MOVE:

Scarlett's move to Korea to train with the best in the world was a radical idea back when she made the move in 2013. Now it's pretty much required for any serious *Starcraft 2* pro!

▶ ZERG RUSH:

While the term "zerg rush" comes from the first *Starcraft* game, the strategy is just as strong as ever in the sequel—and a Scarlett favorite to boot! Just make a ton of zerglings and send them charging at the enemy—they won't know what hit 'em.

▶ KEEPING IT CHEESY:

While they're sometimes frowned upon as unfair, "cheese" strategies are all-or-nothing plays meant to catch your opponent off guard. Be careful when you decide to cheese your opponent, though, because if things go wrong, you might be the one in trouble!

▶ NEVER LET IT GET TO YOUR HEAD:

For some players too much fame can get in the way of playing the game. Not Scarlett, though—when it comes to *Starcraft 2* she's a true professional. "I don't really pay attention as much to whether or not I'm famous or fans or interviews or anything. I just like focusing on the game itself and playing."

CALL IT A COMEBACK

For many pro players taking a break can be downright deadly, but Scarlett isn't most players. In early 2015 she decided to step away from *Starcraft* due to some serious burnout. By that point Scarlett had been playing almost nonstop for five straight years, so it isn't all that surprising that she wanted to take a break. However, it wasn't long before that competitive itch returned and Scarlett found herself back in the spotlight. Most pros would have gotten rusty, but Scarlett came back with a vengeance, posting some of her best tournament finishes of her entire career!

MAJOR VICTORIES

▶ IEM SEASON XII – PYEONGCHANG
▶ WESG 2016 – NORTH & SOUTH AMERICA QUALIFIER
▶ 2012 BATTLE.NET NORTH AMERICAN CHAMPIONSHIP

STARCRAFT MANIA!

Starcraft was one of the very first games that people were able to play professionally, laying the groundwork for what we know today as modern esports. Many things we think of as pretty common in esports—such as teams for single player games, coaches, and gaming houses—all started out as radical ideas in the *Starcraft* professional scene. *Starcraft*'s impact on esports is absolutely massive!

1) In South Korea, there are TV channels that broadcast *Starcraft* matches all day long!

2) Some colleges have offered courses teaching the theory and strategy of professional *Starcraft*.

3) *Starcraft* is used by the United States Air Force to teach new officers how to operate under stressful conditions.

4) An annual conference is held to test out AI in *Starcraft* games against professional human players. Luckily for us, the humans are still winning!

KEY INFO
Developer: Game Freak
Publisher: Nintendo
Release date: September 1998
Genre: RPG
Play it on: Switch, 3DS

POKÉMON

BECOME THE VERY BEST!

CATCH 'EM ALL!

Pokémon is one of the biggest, most successful, and easily recognizable games in the entire world. It's been that way since *Pokémon Red* and *Pokémon Blue* made their debut way back in 1998, and while the games have evolved in the last two decades, the spirit remains the same. As a young Trainer, you undertake an adventure to become the very best, like no one has ever seen. That adventure is split between two primary objectives that work to instill a sense of competition, collaboration, and community in

each and every one of its players. The first goal is for aspirational Trainers attempting to catch and catalog as many Pokémon in a region as humanly possible. The second pushes you to capture, train, and evolve specific Pokémon before then taking them into battles with other Trainers and Gym Leaders. It's no wonder *Pokémon* has become a phenomenon, since it constantly pushes players to meet and share in the sheer joy that is waiting to be found in capturing, training, and battling Pokémon.

DID YOU KNOW?

When the series began, there were only 151 Pokémon to collect. That might sound like a lot, but nowadays there are more than 800!

⭐ HISTORY

POKÉMON RED / BLUE
This is where it all began: the original *Pokémon* game. Everything that makes the series great starts here, and it's still fun to play!

POKÉMON GOLD / SILVER
Considered to be the best that the series has ever been, it's well worth tracking down a copy if you can!

POKÉMON SUN / MOON
Sun and Moon has been the standard competitive *Pokémon* game since its arrival in 2016.

POKÉMON GO!
This game is a global phenomenon, letting you catch Pokémon out in the real world with your smartphone.

POKÉMON LET'S GO, PIKACHU!
If you've never played a *Pokémon* game, *Let's Go, Pikachu!* is a relaxing way to familiarize yourself with the core gameplay.

POKÉMON SWORD / SHIELD
The latest installment to the long-running series, this will be the standard on the competitive scene in 2020 and beyond.

POKÉMON WORLD CHAMPIONSHIPS

So, you've already caught 'em all and are now looking for a new challenge? Then it's about time that you set your sights on the Pokémon World Championships. This annual invitation-only event sees the most skilled Trainers in the world come together and battle it out, both for a cash prize and the opportunity to be dubbed The Very Best—a moniker that, for many *Pokémon* fans, is far more valuable than any monetary offering. Players compete all throughout the year at local events (you can go to the

official *Pokémon* website to see if there's an event near you) against other ambitious Trainers. If they win enough Double Battles they will earn themselves that all-important invite to the World Championships. Winning at these events is all about building a solid strategy, making sure you've put together a well-rounded squad and can be prepared to respond to new challenges quickly. It's competitive, it's fun, and it's one of the very best ways to live the Pokémon dream.

HOW TO QUALIFY

WHAT IT TAKES TO PLAY IN THE *POKÉMON* WORLD CHAMPIONSHIPS

▶ **SQUAD BUILDER**
Put together a squad of your most powerful Pokémon and be ready for anything.

▶ **RULE BOOK**
Familiarize yourself with the rules of PWC on the official *Pokémon* website.

TYPES OF EVENTS

Here's an overview of the different types of competitive *Pokémon* events happening in a city near you, which you'll need to compete in to earn yourself a place in the Pokemon World Championships.

GET PREPARED

ONLINE BATTLES

A great way to test your skills and your squads with little risk; the champions started here once upon a time.

PREMIER CHALLENGES

Local events that can start you on your long journey to become a true *Pokémon* master.

SET YOUR TEAM

You'll want to make sure your squad is ready to go the second you arrive at a tournament, so figure it out the night before and lock it down!

MIDSEASON SHOWDOWN

The place to go when you're ready to take the next step in your Trainer career.

REGIONAL CHAMPIONSHIPS

More challenging than local tournaments, expect a real test to come out victorious.

BUILD STRATEGIES

Ahead of a game starting you'll be able to get a preview of your opponent's team, use this time wisely to begin constructing strategies.

TRACK YOUR TIME

Competitive games run on timers, so you should be aware of how long you're taking to make decisions and try to work on instinct.

INTERNATIONAL CHAMPIONSHIPS

This is an opportunity to test your skills against players from all over the globe and earn huge prizes.

WORLD CHAMPIONSHIPS

Earn enough Championship Points, awarded to top Trainers at every other event, and you'll get an invitation to the World Championships.

HAVE FUN

Remember, becoming a *Pokémon* master is supposed to fun! Take it easy, enjoy the competition, and try to have a good time while you're playing.

▶ **EVENT LOCATOR**
Use the Event Locator to see what opportunities are in your near area.

▶ **CHALLENGE TRAINERS**
Attend local Premier Challenges and Midseason Showdowns to raise your profile.

▶ **DO REGIONALS**
Impress at Regional Championships to earn an invite to the finals.

▶ **WORLD CHAMPS**
This invite-only event sees the best Trainers in the world compete to be the *very* best.

BUILD YOUR TEAM

VARIETY IS KEY

If you want to compete with the best players in the world, you're going to need a squad of Pokémon that's ready to face any surprises thrown your way. The best way to accomplish this is to train Pokémon from a variety of different types—you need to make sure that you have a broad array of resistances in your party to help cover over the major weaknesses. This is key for building a successful squad, although learning to use them properly takes hard work, practice, and experience.

HIGH STATS

If you want to get into fighting shape, be sure to hatch your Pokémon from the Pokémon Day Care Center.

KEEP IT SIMPLE

Try to keep your squad simple. A traditional team will be focused around Grass-type, Fire-type, and Water-type Pokémon.

POPULAR BUILDS

Search for Championship Series Event Results online and look for teams that have proven to be successful recently.

START SMALL

Every Trainer has to start somewhere. When you're happy with your squad, try battling friends and others online before you take it to official events. Competitive experience is always helpful, no matter where you find it.

STATS

$10k
POKÉMON WORLD CHAMPS PRIZE MONEY

1500
COMPETITORS TAKE PART EACH YEAR

636,700
VIEWS OF THE POKÉMON WORLD CHAMPIONSHIPS ON TWITCH

DID YOU KNOW?

The most popular Pokémon on the competitive circuit can indeed change from year to year, but here are just a few of the best from last year.

LANDORUS-THERIAN

This Ground- and Flying-type Pokémon proved popular last year due to its versatile move set. Even if you don't want to use it yourself, you should have a way to counter it in mind: you're sure to face it!

TAPU KOKO ▶

Tapu Koko is an Electric- and Fairy-type Pokémon, a Legendary Pokémon that's great for going on the offensive through its awesome combo of speed, power, and variety of moves.

POPULAR POKÉMON

CHARIZARD

Can't beat a classic. Charizard is number 006 in the Pokédex, the final evolution of original starter Charmander from the first ever game, but it's still the monster to beat in competitive play.

KARTANA ▲

This Grass- and Steel-type Pokémon is one of the most threatening and feared creatures in the competitive game. Its impressive Attack and Speed make it a formidable opponent to face.

TOP TRAINER TIPS

Everything you need to know to get in fighting-ready shape!

TYPE EFFECTIVENESS

Some attacks will do more or less damage depending on the Pokémon you are up against. For example, you wouldn't want to put a Fire-type Pokémon up against a Water-type Pokémon.

SWITCH SMARTLY

You can switch Pokémon out of combat and back to safety at any time, and you should use this to help manage your match-ups throughout a battle.

COMBINE ATTACKS

Double battles are the standard in competitive play, so you should look to combine the abilities of your two fighters to maximize effectiveness.

GLOSSARY

IV
Individual Values is a hidden stat that's important for competitive Trainers.

EV
Effort Values are tied to each stat in the game, improving as you use and battle with your Pokémon.

MOVE
These are the attacks and defensive maneuvers you can use in battle.

ABILITIES
Passive effects that can appear in battle or in the overworld.

SHINY POKÉMON

These hyper-rare Pokémon have a sparkling animation, denoting that they are "Shiny." These variants have the best stats in the game, so be on the lookout for one!

THE BATTLE BEGINS

Pokémon is an easy game to learn, but it's challenging to master! If you want to improve at the game you'll need to stick with it, rotating out your team of Pokémon and trying new tactics in battle—especially before you start going up against other Trainers online or in the wild. The important thing is to look for good combinations of Pokémon types and to keep a close eye on what Pokémon your rival is choosing to unleash. The more you play the more you will come to understand!

1 MOVE SET
Be mindful of the moves at your disposal and your opponent's weaknesses.

2 CHANGE UP
Don't be afraid to switch Pokémon out of battle if they are getting beaten.

3 USE ITEMS
In your bag you'll find a number of useful items that can turn the tide in battle.

4 BE MINDFUL
This shows how many active Pokémon your opponent has remaining.

Catch With Care

CHOOSE WISELY
Not every creature is worth capturing!

BUILD SOLID COMBOS
Fill gaps in your team.

TRAIN HARD
Spread XP evenly around your team.

KEY INFO
Developer: Riot Games
Publisher: Riot Games
Release date: October 2009
Genre: MOBA
Play it on: PC

LEAGUE OF LEGENDS

RIOT'S GLOBAL MOBA PHENOMENON!

STEP ONTO SUMMONER'S RIFT

In the ten years since its launch, few games have become a global craze like *League of Legends*. This multiplayer online battle arena game is the essence of the genre! It features intense five-versus-five combat, deep strategy with colorful and exciting Champions, and plenty of ways to get ahead—or fall behind! Each game is unique: You choose from more than 140 characters, pick a role, and fight across the map to devastate your enemy's base.

The passion of millions of players has given *LoL* one of the most immense and exciting official esports communities around. Alongside their teams, players compete locally and travel to events to prove they're the best. Even if you don't want to fight your way to the top, *LoL* is a popular hobby for millions. You can play with friends, go at it solo, and even stream your climb to the top online. It may be intimidating to start learning, but that's what makes the challenge fun!

DID YOU KNOW?

If playing with one Champion is getting dull, don't fear. There are 146 to choose from— and the roster is always growing!

⭐ MAP OBJECTIVES

FIRST BLOOD
Scoring the first successful attack on another player will earn you bonus gold, so get in there quick!

FIRST TURRET
This refers to the first time one team destroys another's defensive turret. More gold for you!

DRAGONS
Defeating one of these three beasties will provide a very useful teamwide power boost.

ELDER DRAGON
Boosts other dragon boosts and makes your team attack harder and faster.

RIFT HERALD
Provides Recall cooldown boost— and a summonable allied Rift Herald.

BARON NASHOR
Killing this monster gives the ultimate massive range of teamwide power boosts.

DID YOU KNOW?
Team Liquid won the North American 2019 League of Legends Championship.

WORLDS-WIDE COMPETITION

League of Legends' competitive scene soared even in its early days, before it became one of the giants of the modern esports scene. Nowadays, there are opportunities all over the globe to become a legendary player —and the best of the best have their eyes on Worlds, the year-end championship title.

Throughout the year, teams play in one of numerous official leagues based on their region. There are five major leagues with guaranteed Worlds slots: three in Asia, one in Europe, and one in North America. Nine smaller "play-in" regions around the globe also allow teams to fight their way to Worlds. Along the way, they must take on other play-in regions and, eventually, certain major league teams.

At Worlds, these teams come together to determine the year's reigning champion. Millions of viewers watch weeks of intense competition culminate in the Worlds Finals, one of the most anticipated days of esports each year. Every year, new legends are forged!

A YEAR IN LEAGUE
HOW *LOL*'S INTENSE PRO SEASON FITS TOGETHER

▶ **SPRING SPLIT**
This is the first part of the regular *LoL* tournament season.

▶ **SUMMER SPLIT**
Determines who will get locked in for Worlds.

▶ **PLAY-INS**
Play-in and third-place teams battle for the last Worlds spots.

LEAGUES OF LEAGUE

In League esports, players who do well in public games are recruited into teams in one of many leagues. The best of the best will often find themselves in the official leagues run by Riot Games themselves. It's quite the honor—and super competitive!

NORTH AMERICA
Fan-favorite teams like Team SoloMid compete in the North American League of Legends Championship Series. Places in the LCS are hotly contested as new challengers rise!

KOREA
This region hosts the famous League of Legends Champions Korea (LCK) series. Many of the greatest teams in the history of *LoL* originated in Korea—make it here, and you can make it anywhere!

CHINA
The League of Legends Pro League hosts a robust roster of Chinese teams. The LPL produces talented squads that are capable of going all the way to the top of the championship—as was the case in 2018!

EUROPE
Europeans battle in the European League of Legends Championships (EU LCS). The first-ever Worlds champions came from Europe, but the trophy has never returned—will this year change all that?

TAIWAN, HONG KONG, MACAO
League Masters Series represents these Southeast Asian countries. *League of Legends* is very popular here, making it a hotbed for new talent—never count an LMS team out!

GLOBAL
Plenty more regions around the world have official leagues! The LCL covers Russia and CIS countries, while the OCS covers Oceania. There are opportunities to compete in pro *LoL* all over the world!

HISTORIC TEAMS

SK TELECOM T1
Headed by world famous pro Lee "Faker" Sang-hyeok, the Korean squad won three consecutive Worlds championships!

INVICTUS GAMING
After years of being a legendary Chinese esports organization, the team won the first Worlds title for their region in 2018.

FNATIC
This team has performed consistently well in Europe and at Worlds, becoming a staple in both *League of Legends* and the esports world.

TEAM SOLOMID
These North American fan favorites formed from a *League* fan site and have always showed up in the top three of the region.

▶ **WORLDS GROUPS**
Teams battle in the early stages of the Worlds championships.

▶ **WORLDS PLAYOFFS**
The remaining teams make one final push in order to reach the Worlds summit!

PUSHING THE WIN

EARLY FARM

In *League of Legends*, you "farm" or collect gold for items and experience, which leads to new abilities and powers as time goes on. That means you need to get off to a strong start! Like running a race, if you and your teammates are too far behind early on, it gets hard to catch up and win. But as time goes on, you'll find more ways to close the gap. You start by defeating small computer-controlled creatures in each lane called "minions" and collecting their gold and experience.

WELCOME TO THE JUNGLE

The jungler defeats monsters so that their allies can focus on minions—but they need to keep an eye out for enemies, too!

GANK TIME!

When players are powerful enough, they need to team up to "gank" or defeat enemy Champions in other lanes!

MAP OBJECTIVES

Both teams want to grab Drakes, Rift Heralds, and Baron Nashor to catch up from a setback—or stay ahead!

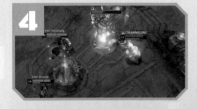

INTO THE BASE

Eventually, of course, your team needs to push down all of the enemy team's turrets and get into their base. After defeating the defenders, destroy the Nexus to win the game!

STATS

44 MILLION
▶ VIEWERS DURING WORLDS 2018 GRAND FINALS

$2,418,750
WORLDS 2018 GRAND PRIZE

24
TEAMS ATTENDING WORLDS 2018

BASE SWEET BASE

NEXUS
The goal of the game is to protect yours and destroy theirs. Keep your eyes on it—minions can win a game for you or your enemies!

INHIBITOR
When your team destroys these, your minions become a bit stronger. Use it to your advantage, but be careful, because they rebuild themselves!

DID YOU KNOW?
Musical guests for official *LoL* tunes have included rock band Imagine Dragons, EDM artists Zedd and The Glitch Mob, and K-pop group G-Idle!

TURRET
These structures attack nearby enemies. They're scattered throughout the map, but, of course, the ones protecting your base are going to save your life—and Nexus.

FOUNTAIN
This is a multipurpose stop. It's where you spawn and buy items, but you can also automatically heal by stepping in at any time.

KEEP AN EYE OUT

Make sure you stay safe in the Rift with these helpful hints and tips!

WATCH THE MINI-MAP

Everyone you can see will show up here. If you can't see every enemy, be careful!

DON'T WANDER

If you wander too far, the enemy will catch you on their side of the map!

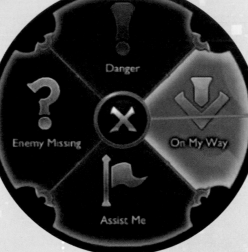

WARD YOUR LANES

Your support should put up wards so you can catch the enemy trying to sneak around.

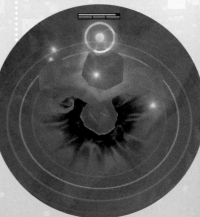

COMMUNICATE

Use the game's ping system, which allows you to point out potential dangers across the map.

BUDDY SYSTEM

Not sure if an enemy is nearby? Ask a teammate if they'll go with you.

ROLES TO PLAY

Much like any large team sport, every player has a role to play. Each role comes with its own set of responsibilities. For instance, most players need as much gold as possible, but the support is also tasked with making sure their teammates don't die. The jungler and mid frequently move around to take down enemies. Every bit of help counts!

1 ADC
While weak at the start, these players become heavy hitters before the end.

2 MID
Bold and attentive, the solo mid player is likely to grow in power quickly.

3 TOP
Brave go-getters, these players tough it out on their own—much like mids.

4 JUNGLE
Junglers defeat creatures and occasionally help teammates out by attacking the other team to scare them off. Gotta be tough to survive in the wilds of the jungle!

5 SUPPORT
Supports watch over the ADC, making sure the enemy doesn't try anything funny. With early-game power and perks, they're a perfect farming companion!

Ability Types

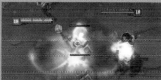

ACTIVE
Your character's main abilities require a press of a button!

PASSIVE
This activates without pressing buttons. Set it and don't worry.

ULTIMATE
Your heavy-hitter. Save this for special moments like teamfights!

DOTA 2

BIG GAME, BIG MONEY!

KEY INFO
Developer: Valve
Publisher: Valve
Release date: July 2013
Genre: MOBA
Play it on: PC

THE ORIGINAL MOBA

With ever-changing gameplay, a long legacy in esports, and tournaments with unimaginable amounts of money at stake, *Dota 2* ticks all the boxes as a classic esports game. It started life in 2002 as *Defense of the Ancients*, a fan-made game mode for Blizzard's *WarCraft III*. *Dota 2* is a remake, created by Valve Software with help from some of the game's original developers.

Two teams of five choose one of 117 characters, and each team fights its way into opposing territory to destroy the enemy

Ancient. The players must destroy smaller creatures and towers, earn gold to spend on items, and avoid being caught by the enemy team. With so many characters, more than 160 items and a sprawling battlefield, it can take years to learn how to play. But with a massive annual tournament called The International —worth more than $25 million in 2018—there's always motivation to keep trying! *Dota 2* has made more millionaires than any other esport.

★ AROUND THE MAP

CREEPS
Creeps appear every 30 seconds. They'll fight each other until heroes get involved!

COURIER
This creature can bring you items while you're far from home, as long as it stays safe!

SECRET SHOPS
Powerful items are sold within, but you'll need to go out of your way to reach it!

ANCIENT CREEPS
Larger, more powerful neutral enemies that offer big rewards!

RUNES
Earn short special boosts by grabbing these gems before the enemy can snatch them!

ROSHAN
Defeating this monster will give your team gold, experience, and an instant revive item.

HEROIC ROLES

While *Dota 2* has endless strategic possibilities, most players structure their teams around how much gold each character earns.

OFFLANER

Requiring a tough skin or a nimble escape ability, the offlaner holds its ground against multiple enemies while trying to earn a little gold.

MID-LANER

"Mids" are the most open to attack by other players, but left to their own devices, they quickly become powerful adversaries early in the game.

CARRY

Carries earn the most gold and buy the most items in order to become the toughest players later in the game. They must be protected at all costs!

GLOSSARY

FARMING
Earning gold and experience by taking out creeps and neutral enemies.

TALENT TREE
Player-chosen upgrades to abilities and character statistics. Choose wisely!

DENY
Destroying your own creeps so the enemy can't earn the full reward.

INITIATE
Starting a battle, often by stunning or slowing the enemy down. Go in now!

SUPPORT

Supports roam around the map to help secure team goals and sabotage the enemy. They earn the least gold, but can change the tide of battle with their powerful abilities.

DOTA 2

ENTER THE BATTLEFIELD

Every time you start a game of *Dota 2*, many things will change: You'll need to pick from a large pool of characters, make quick decisions about items, and adapt around everyone's choices. What remains consistent across each game is the battlefield, known as the map.

The map features many secrets that you can use to your advantage. For example, using wards in certain spots can help you see enemies before they know they've been spotted. Plus, hiding behind trees and up hills can make you temporarily invisible to enemies, so they can't click on you!

Each side of the map has a unique layout. However, in order to keep the game fair, both have several key features in common.

1 BASE
Where the Ancient must be defended! Come back to the fountain to heal.

2 SAFE LANE
The longer lane on your side, where your carry will earn most of their gold.

3 MID LANE
The shortest route between the two bases—this area is often highly contested!

4 JUNGLE
Dangerous territory where neutral enemies can be hunted by heroes on the move.

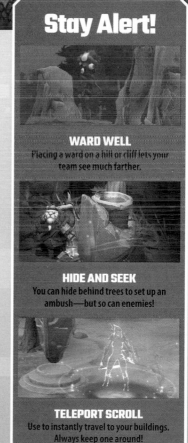

Stay Alert!

WARD WELL
Placing a ward on a hill or cliff lets your team see much farther.

HIDE AND SEEK
You can hide behind trees to set up an ambush—but so can enemies!

TELEPORT SCROLL
Use to instantly travel to your buildings. Always keep one around!

KUROKY

KEY FACTS

Name: Kuro "KuroKy" Takhasomi
Origin: Iran (born), Germany (raised)
Company: Team Liquid
Games played: *Defense of the Ancients, Dota 2*
Playing since: 2008

uroKy is a professional *Dota 2* player who has been part of the esports scene for over a decade. KuoKy began his professional *Dota 2* career in 2011 when he played in the very first *Dota 2* world championship, The International 2011, for team GosuGamer.net. Since then, KuroKy has become one of the most successful *Dota 2* players the game has ever seen, boasting dozens of Top 8 tournament finishes and even a victory at The International 2017. Always looking to improve, KuroKy won't rest until he is recognized as the indisputable best to ever play the game!

PRO TIPS

▶ **JACK OF ALL TRADES:**

Having a big hero pool in *Dota 2* is important, but KuroKy takes it to the next level—he's played over 100 unique heroes in professional games!

▶ **I THINK I'LL FLEX A BIT:**

KuroKy has found success as both a carry and a support. Being able to excel in multiple positions is hard for even some of the best pros, but it can take your game to the next level.

▶ **A CAPTAIN GOES DOWN WITH HIS SHIP:**

While KuroKy didn't start out as team leader, his hard work and great attitude allowed him to eventually become a captain capable of leading his team to victory!

▶ **IT'S ALL IN THE MIND:**

What's one of the biggest keys to esports success? According to KuroKy, you've got to keep a clear head. "The mental preparation is the main part of esports overall I think, be it *DOTA* or any other game . . . it's just about being stable."

A TRUE TEAM PLAYER

With a career as long as KuroKy's, it comes as no surprise that he has played on a bunch of different teams. While he really got his start on Team Mousesports, KuroKy has played for Virtus.pro, Na'Vi, and even formed his own team called Team Secret. While he has been a powerhouse on each roster, it truly has been on Team Liquid, his current team, that KuroKy has found the most success. But who knows, it might not be long before KuroKy finds a whole new team—and a whole new way to dominate *Dota 2*!

MAJOR VICTORIES

- ▶ THE INTERNATIONAL 2017
- ▶ CHINA *DOTA 2* SUPERMAJOR
- ▶ EPICENTER 2016

PAYDAY!

The International 2019 set the record for the largest prize pool in the history of esports with a total prize pool $34,292,588! That's almost $10,000,000 more than the next largest . . . The International 2018. In fact, the Top 5 largest prize pools in esports are all from *Dota 2* championship tournaments:

1) The International 2019 $34,292,599.00
2) The International 2018 $25,532,177.00
3) The International 2017 $24,687,919.00
4) The International 2016 $20,770,460.00
5) The International 2015 $18,429,613.00

KEY INFO
Developer: Super Evil Megacorp
Publisher: Super Evil Megacorp
Release date: November 2014
Genre: MOBA
Play it on: PC, Android, iOS

VAINGLORY

MULTI-PLATFORM MOBA MAGIC!

THE MOBILE MOBA!

Super Evil Megacorp's *Vainglory* is one of the first MOBA games to be played competitively on smartphones and tablets: As well as Steam, it's available via the Android and Apple app stores. In *Vainglory*, two teams of five powerful warriors battle across a three-lane map in an attempt to push their army forward and destroy the enemy base. Computer-controlled minions spawn from each side of the map and it's up to the players to use their heroes to push down each lane, attack the enemy team's defensive towers, and eventually destroy their base.

Heroes start out weak, but as the game goes on they will level up and gain new abilities. By purchasing items, players can modify their characters to make them stronger or even change their roles entirely! Individual play is important, but teamwork is even more so. To come out ahead, players must master not only their own hero's abilities, but also how to use them in perfect coordination with their allies.

DID YOU KNOW?

Vainglory's early success was largely thanks to its massive popularity in Indonesia!

 **HEROS OF** *VAINGLORY*

YATES
Yates can pull enemy heroes with his flail, letting his team catch them out of position.

LANCE
The heavily armored Lance spends a recharging stamina meter to perform attacks.

GRUMPJAW
An angry dog-frog-gorilla creature, Grumpjaw is capable of swallowing other heroes!

CELESTE
With control of the stars, Celeste deals massive damage to her foes from afar.

REZA
A flame-wielding mage, Reza can unleash an inner demonic form on anyone foolish enough to get in his way.

LORELAI
Lorelai creates pools of water that speed up allies and power up her future attacks.

MASTER THE MAP

Understanding and controlling the map will let you outwit and outplay your opponents.

SCOUT CAMS

Clear the fog of war by planting Scout cams on common pathways. Keep an eye on enemy movements to avoid ganks and catch out lone heroes. Remember, knowledge is power.

THE RIVER

Following the river's flow from the middle lane to the top or bottom will increase your speed, letting you launch sudden attacks. This makes control of the middle lane extremely powerful.

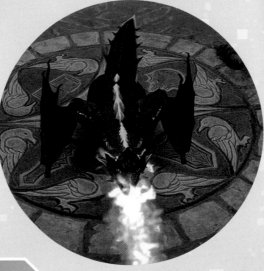

BLACKCLAW & GHOSTWING

Take down these mighty creatures with your team to gain powerful rewards. Blackclaw will launch an attack on the middle lane, while Ghostwing gives your team healing shields.

GLOSSARY

WP
WP usually refers to a hero's default, auto-attack damage.

CP
CP typically refers to a hero's ability and spell damage.

PEEL
Pulling enemies off a teammate so that they can escape.

KITE
Alternating attacking and running with a ranged hero to keep your distance.

RIVER SHOP

Instead of returning to base, save time by visiting the river shop in your lane. The items you buy there can change the tide of battle, but it's also a prime spot for an ambush.

LANES AND MAP POSITIONS

Vainglory's map is split into three lanes that players fight over. The map is mirrored so that both sides see themselves as playing from left to right (your bottom lane is the opponent's top lane). Knowing your role and place is important, since putting too many players in one area leaves weaknesses elsewhere.

Each lane needs at least one player to attack and defend it, leaving two remaining roles. Most teams have a jungler (a player who kills neutral monsters between lanes) whose job is to build up experience and money for the late game. The final player is usually the team captain who plays a support role, assisting players on the main lanes.

1

TOP/BOTTOM LANE

Lone heroes usually play in top or bottom. Top usually has the least support.

2

MIDDLE LANE

The most valuable lane. The captain usually supports here, rotating to top or bottom when needed.

3

JUNGLE

One player farms money and experience here, supporting a bottom lane damage dealer.

Heroic Tips

TALK TO YOUR TEAM

Regularly inform your team of you and your opponent's movements.

KNOW YOUR STRENGTHS

Some heroes excel in the late game, while others are perfect early assassins.

DENY THEIR INCOME

Killing your own minions stops the enemy from earning money.

STREET FIGHTER V

OLD-SCHOOL'S STILL COOL!

PERFECT KO!

In the history of fighting games, few series have had as much of an impact as *Street Fighter*—whole generations of competitive gamers have been shaped by different versions of this arcade classic. The first *Street Fighter* focused on the one-player adventure mode rather than fighting against friends, but many are familiar with the one-versus-one arcade versions that came later. It was common for gamers to take on their friends after school, or simply practice against the bots and beat the story mode. Developer Capcom released sequel after sequel with new characters, new worldwide locations, and more.

Street Fighter remains one of the core games of the fighting game community—the players that follow one-versus-one fighting games, old and new. It's simple enough: Players take on an opponent in a beat-'em-up match using a character from a colorful roster.

You can take on others online or in-person—and with enough practice, you can become the ultimate fighting champion!

DID YOU KNOW?

While *Street Fighter* has five main games, there are many editions—there have been at least 35 *Street Fighter* games over the decades!

⭐ SHOW YOUR MOVES

ATTACK
You punch or kick at different intensities—light, medium, or hard—and your movement determines if it's high, center, or low.

BLOCK
Press the movement button away from your enemy to block multiple enemy attacks. But beware: Some moves can't be blocked!

DASH
Double-tap your movement button left or right to quickly move toward or away from your opponent.

JUMP
Jump to dodge an attack, move around, or set up a special midair attack of your own!

CROUCH
You can crouch to dodge a high attack, or set up your own strike from below. Catch your opponent off guard!

SPECIAL
If you press the correct set of buttons, your character will unleash one of their unique Special attacks, like Ryu's Hadouken.

CAPCOM PRO TOUR

For decades, dedicated *Street Fighter* players have competed against one another, whether in the arcades, at school events, or in garages. In the '90s with *Street Fighter II* and in the 2000s with *Street Fighter III*, tournaments took place all over the world. Now, however, those who have been training all these years have a chance to prove their worth with the official Capcom Pro Tour.

The Capcom Pro Tour is a series of tournaments sponsored by the game's publisher. These lead up to an end-of-year final tournament called the Capcom Cup. Anyone is allowed to enter and try to come out on top! Players either win certain events or earn points at sponsored tournaments to be invited to the Capcom Cup. Of course, the competition is not easy, but players from all regions and of all ages have proven to be worthy opponents. The winner in 2018, a Japanese player named Gachikun, took home $250,000. Train to be the best and there's more than just money on the line—there's enduring glory, too!

LEGACY OF STREET FIGHTER

HOW THIS LEGENDARY GAME HAS EVOLVED OVER THE YEARS

▶ 1987
The first game introduced Ryu and Ken as the main characters of the series.

▶ 1991
SFII introduced the option to battle with more characters.

CLASSIC CHARACTERS RUMBLE AGAIN!

Part of what's made the *Street Fighter* series so memorable across generations are the interesting (and sometimes hilarious) characters that you can pick. Everyone has their favorites—which is your main?

RYU
This iconic character is a balanced pick and a great way for new players to learn the basics.

KEN
Ryu's friendly rival, Ken, has shorter range but stronger attacks. He favors an aggressive style!

CHUN-LI
This quick fighter can get plenty of jabs in on the enemy—and follow up with devastating kicks!

M. BISON
The villain of the series is a dangerous opponent. Watch out for his dashing and diving special attacks!

ZANGIEF
This macho wrestler is most known for his throwing technique. He's pretty slow, though!

GUILE
Patience is the name of the game with Guile, but charge up his powerful specials and it'll pay off.

CAMMY
Speedy but simple Cammy is great for patient players who can set up impactful counterattacks.

BLANKA
This madcap fighter leaps around and tackles his opponent with unique lightning moves!

AKUMA
While Akuma packs raw attack power, he's very weak on defense. Go all out to win!

SAKURA
Don't underestimate her—Sakura packs some powerful combos when she gets in close.

▶ 1997
Street Fighter's third iteration became a major tournament staple.

▶ 2008
Street Fighter IV arrives in time to be part of the rise of esports.

▶ 2017
The latest version, *SFV*, includes online play for the modern esports era.

SFV'S NEW V-SYSTEM

WHAT'S THE V-SYSTEM?
A new system of skills unique to each character.

V-SKILL
Usable at any time, the V-Skill is a short but useful ability.

V-REVERSAL
The V-Reversal uses your V-Gauge bar to counter opponents' attacks.

V-TRIGGER
V-Trigger drains your V-Gauge to gain extra power for a short time.

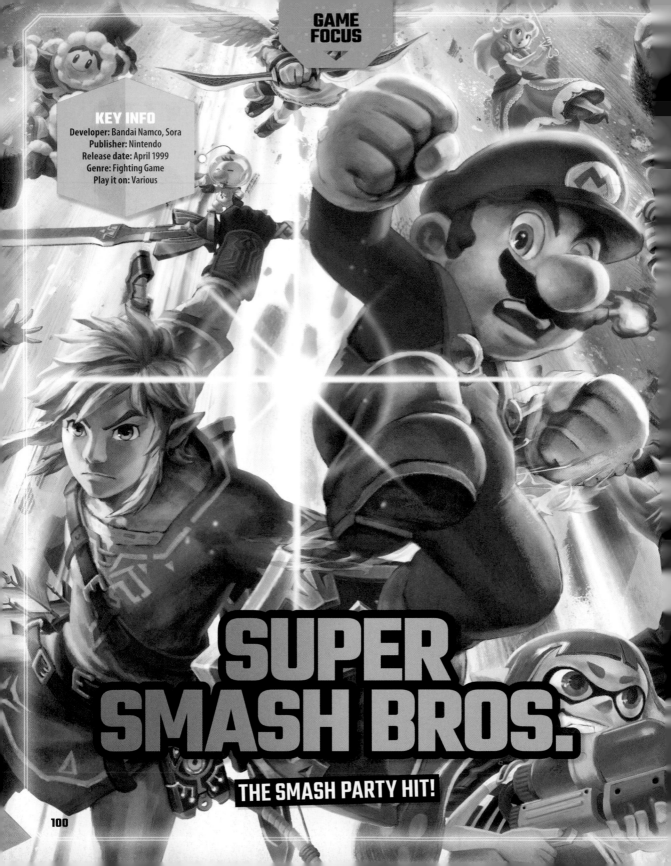

KEY INFO
Developer: Bandai Namco, Sora
Publisher: Nintendo
Release date: April 1999
Genre: Fighting Game
Play it on: Various

SUPER SMASH BROS.

THE SMASH PARTY HIT!

ALL-STAR RUMBLE!

Have you ever seen Mario take on Bowser? Peach versus Koopa? How about Link against Samus? Maybe Pac-Man versus Kirby, or *Street Fighter*'s Ryu versus Pikachu? You can only find these sorts of battles in *Super Smash Bros*. The classic battle series brings together some of the most iconic characters in video gaming history for serious smackdowns. Take on another player solo, or battle with up to eight people on a single stage. And if you're really feeling like having fun, there are hundreds of usable items and "Assist Trophies," which summon characters from other popular games to help you out!

For more than twenty years, this game has remained a staple at parties and events. And it's easy to see why: Each playable character is unique and brings cool abilities to the table. Whether it's Wario's motorbike, Ken or Ryu's Hadouken, or Jigglypuff's sleepy song, you have a massive arsenal of powerful moves to unleash. It's the ultimate gaming crossover battle!

⭐ SHOW YOUR MOVES

NEUTRAL
Your basic attack can be aimed in eight directions. Simple but effective.

SMASH
A more impactful hit. Charge up a Smash attack to do more damage!

SPECIAL
Your character's unique abilities are called "Specials." Each one is different!

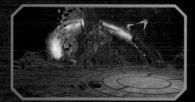

JUMP
Jumping lets you move between platforms to get the drop on your foe!

DODGE
Slide out of the way when your enemy attacks, but be careful not to leave yourself open!

SHIELD
Blocks some damage, but beware! Take too many hits and you'll freeze for a few seconds.

SMASH HISTORY

SUPER SMASH BROS.

Released in 1999, this Nintendo 64 hit got attention for bringing together some of the biggest names in gaming at the time. Sixteen characters were playable in this version, four of which had to be unlocked through gameplay. Combined with the popularity of the N64, it became a huge hit and a staple at sleepovers, parties, and after-school hangouts. To this day, some events put together special tournaments to honor the legacy of the original *Smash Bros.* game.

BRAWL

This Wii version is much loved for introducing non-Nintendo characters like Solid Snake and Megaman.

MELEE

The GameCube edition, which has 26 characters, is still a staple at all major Smash Bros. tournaments.

4 FOR WIIU/DS

While the WiiU was less popular than the N64 or Switch, this version was still a hit!

ULTIMATE

The current edition of *Smash Bros.* is the biggest one yet, with dozens of new characters and a focus on competitive play that makes running tournaments easy. There's a character for everyone!

STATS

SEVENTY-ONE FIGHTERS PLAYABLE IN ULTIMATE

104 STAGES AVAILABLE TO BATTLE ON

39 GAME-CHANGING ASSIST TROPHIES TO BE SUMMONED!

MAKE YOUR MOVE

Every *Smash* character is defined by their Specials, and Kirby is no different!

SIDE: HAMMER FLIP
Send your foes flying with a powerful hammer attack!

UP: FINAL CUTTER
Jump up with a sword, then land and send out a shockwave!

DOWN: STONE
Turn into a stone to slam down and hit enemies below you!

B ONLY: INHALE
Inhale another fighter and borrow their Specials!

STEP UP
YOUR SMASH

These hints will help you become a better competitive *Smash* player!

EYES ON THE ENEMY

A popular tip from pros is to keep your eyes on the enemy instead of your own fighter, so that you don't get caught by surprise!

MAKE SOME FRIENDS

Do your friends play *Smash*? The best way to learn is to play with a friend! If not, start out by learning against tough computer opponents. Then, consider online play!

BUILD A COMBO

A combo is when you use attacks in a certain order to make sure your enemy can't counterattack. Experiment to find your own!

GLOSSARY

AERIAL
An attack done in the air. Most attacks and Specials can be performed in this way.

EDGE GUARDING
After an enemy has fallen off the stage, edge guarding helps keep them away!

MAIN
Your "main" is your most frequent fighter pick—your go-to against tough foes!

SELF-DESTRUCT
Accidentally falling off the stage. Don't worry—it happens to everybody.

PICK YOUR MAIN

Don't get overwhelmed! Pick a character (or two) you like and learn to play them well. Having a main is how the pros rise to the top!

SUPER SMASH BROS.

④

②

①

③

15.2%
MARIO

0.0%
LINK

24
INKLI

0%
ONG

IN THE MELEE

When you and your friends step onto the *Super Smash Bros.* battlefield, it can be a little overwhelming. In addition to each player's character and their flashy Specials, you've got to pay attention to the stages themselves— they're always moving, and changing, and presenting new challenges. Top-level *Smash* players are capable of paying attention to everything that's going on—which is easier said than done!

Each *Smash* battle boils down to a few key elements that you should always try to pay attention to.

① PORTRAIT
That's you! Custom costumes and colors help you stand out from the crowd.

② SPECIAL
Specials interact with the environment in different ways. Mario's fireball bounces!

③ DAMAGE
The more damage a character takes, the farther they get knocked back by hits!

④ PLATFORMS
You can move—or attack—through most floating platforms. Attack from below!

Top Advice

KEEP YOUR DISTANCE
Some abilities work at a distance. Build up their damage!

HIDDEN HURT
Specials can look less harmful than they actually are. Experiment!

JUMP AROUND
Jumping and up-specials may not be the only way to save yourself!

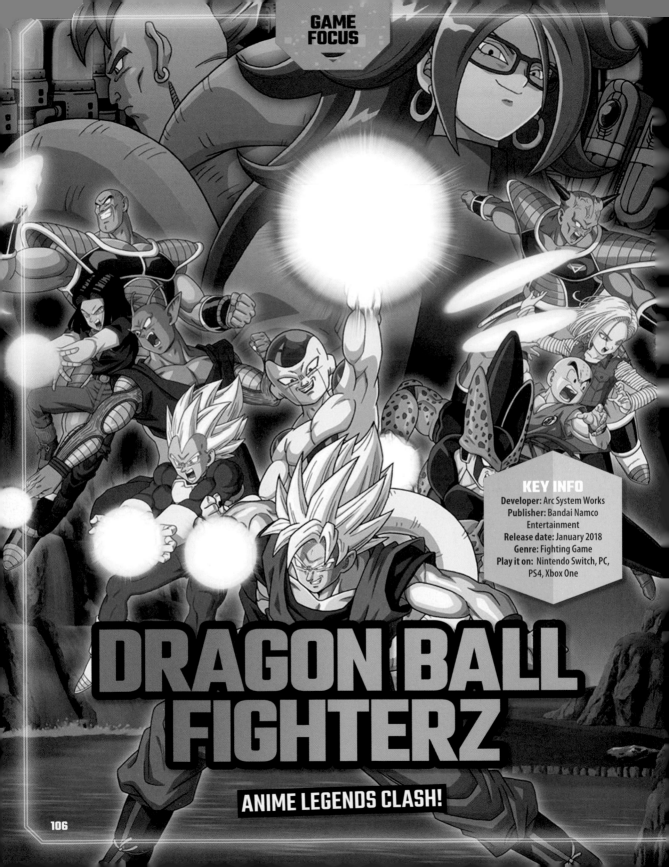

KEY INFO

Developer: Arc System Works
Publisher: Bandai Namco Entertainment
Release date: January 2018
Genre: Fighting Game
Play it on: Nintendo Switch, PC, PS4, Xbox One

DRAGON BALL FIGHTERZ

ANIME LEGENDS CLASH!

NEVER GIVE UP!

When you're watching *Dragon Ball*, it's all about the epic battles! Maybe you've seen Goku versus Vegeta, Vegito versus Super Buu, or the crew versus Freiza. But what about Broly versus Krillin, Gotenks versus Android 16, or even Yamcha versus Android 21? *Dragon Ball FighterZ* allows you to create exciting matches where not just one, but three of your favorite legends take on another team of three in a high-stakes royal rumble.

When you play as any character, you get to borrow some of their moves: Goku's Kamehameha, Broly's Eraser Cannon, and Krillin's Destructo-Disc. As with any *Dragon Ball* battle, as the match goes on, the stakes get higher. Charge up Ki to unlock key moves, dash into your enemies with Dragon Rush, and have your team jump in for awesome team attacks. And when you've become powerful enough, you can collect all seven Dragon Balls and unleash massive boosts—but you can't just wish for victory. It needs to be earned through skill, tactics, and determination!

⭐ SPECIAL MOVES

SUPER DASH
Dash into your opponents for a chance to avoid Ki attacks and get a hit in!

ASSIST
A teammate jumps in to help, whether by attacking or blocking.

REFLECT
A block that reacts differently on success, absorbs Ki, and knocks back opponents.

VANISH
Teleport behind your enemy and try to get a quick attack on them!

DRAGON RUSH
This is a dashing throw that lets you catch your opponents off-guard!

SPARKING BLAST
A comeback move that lets you recover health while knocking back your foe.

STAY SHARP, SAIYAN!

Hone your *Dragon Ball* skills!

BALANCE YOUR KI

As in the anime, Ki is a source of energy for your character. You can earn it by acting, and use it for certain moves. Or, charge it on your own!

JUMP AROUND

Learning how to jump and do combos in the air will give you plenty of opportunities to deal a ton of damage to your opponents!

PRACTICE COMBOS

DBFZ allows you to use an Auto Combo, which hits your opponent repeatedly. Making a combo can inflict damage, knock enemies into the air, and more!

UNLEASH SUPER ATTACKS

Got a ton of Ki stored up? When three bars of Ki are available, don't forget to use a Super Attack. It'll charge back up quickly, so make sure you take advantage of it.

MEANS TO ENDS

Collecting the Dragon Balls, pulling off Finishers, and doing Super Attacks are cool, but the goal isn't to look cool—it's to defeat your opponent. Don't lose focus, Saiyan!

GLOSSARY

DYNAMIC
A set of moves that grant a random Dragon Ball.

SMASH
Very heavy attack unique to *DBFZ* that knocks back opponents.

SUPER JUMP
A special jump that gives you extra vertical height.

TECH
Quick reaction move done to get out of a sticky situation.

3 POWER UNLEASHED

There's never a truly dull match in *Dragon Ball FighterZ*. To start, there's a massive cast of characters from the *Dragon Ball* series. Each fighter's eye-catching abilities are crafted to look like they're lifted from the cartoons, making every match feel like your own episode.

In each battle, though, don't get too distracted by the exciting visuals! Around the screen, the game gives plenty to keep your eye on that tells you who's capable of what. There are certainly the standard fighting game essentials, but *Dragon Ball FighterZ*'s many quirks are indicated around the screen.

1 BLUE HEALTH
Characters who aren't in play earn some recoverable health back over time. Recoverable health is dark blue.

2 KI
Like a battery for many of your special moves! You can charge up your Ki by performing an Energy Charge move.

3 SPARKING BLAST
Is your super-boost ready to help you stage a comeback? Look for the icon underneath your health bar!

4 DRAGON BALLS
Doing a default auto-combo or landing 100 hits with a combo will earn a Dragon Ball. Earn all seven for a wish!

Key Wishes

BRING BACK MY ALLY!
Restores a knocked-out ally to half-health.

RESTORE MY HEALTH!
Gives you your full health bar back.

MAKE ME IMMORTAL!
Your health always generates to half. Don't let them hit fast!

HALO

THE ALL-CONQUERING SHOOTER SERIES!

KEY INFO
Developer: Bungie, 343 Industries
Publisher: Microsoft
Release date: November 2011
Genre: FPS
Play it on: Xbox One, PC

COMBAT EVOLVED

For almost twenty years, the *Halo* series has stood proud as the pinnacle of FPS gaming on console. Whole generations of gamers have earned their competitive gaming stripes in intense, skillful, and strategic battles between teams of rival Spartan supersoldiers.

This is a game of fast-paced action with a whole armory of sci-fi weapons to bring into battle—players need to master precise movement and develop a deadeye aim to get ahead. Even so, *Halo* distinguishes itself as a shooter series by providing lots of room for strategy, too. In a gunfight, you have to understand how to coordinate your firepower to take down your opponent's shields. In a team match, you'll need good communication and finely developed instincts to outplay the enemy team, claim vital objectives, and win.

The *Halo* series established many of the ideas that FPS gamers now take for granted —and with *Halo Infinite* due in 2020, the future is very bright indeed! If you've never discovered the majesty of competitive *Halo*, now's the time.

DID YOU KNOW?

As well as the games, the *Halo* story has been told through novels, comic books, films, and even anime.

⭐ SPARTAN ARMORY

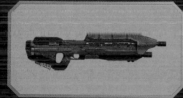

ASSAULT RIFLE
Control your fire to get the most out of this classic weapon at medium range.

BATTLE RIFLE
The three-shot burst from this marksman's weapon can deal serious damage.

CARBINE
The Covenant Carbine is a great medium range weapon that favors a steady aim.

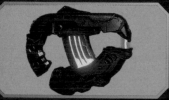

PLASMA PISTOL
When fully charged, the plasma pistol can lower an opponent's shield in one hit!

MAGNUM
Lethal if their shields are down— combine with the plasma pistol for a classic combo.

PLASMA GRENADE
These sticky grenades are a *Halo* staple. Land a direct hit for maximum results!

FIGHT LIKE THE CHIEF

Tips for performing better in *Halo* multiplayer.

USE VEHICLES WISELY

It can be tempting to leap into the cockpit of a flyer or tank, but be careful—they make for a big target!

PUNCH IT UP!

Don't be afraid to throw out a melee attack—if your opponent's shields are down, a strike can be devastating.

PICK YOUR BATTLES

Seek out the optimal engagement range for your weapons—snipers should always seek distance.

LAY OF THE LAND

Halo maps combine narrow winding routes with wide-open areas: Try to fight where the terrain gives you a competitive edge.

GLOSSARY

FORGE
Halo's map editor; used to create custom arenas and game modes.

BOARDING
The act of climbing onto an enemy vehicle and claiming it for yourself.

BOUNCING
Using rocket or grenade blasts to deflect incoming projectiles.

FACE PAINTING
Firing while dragging your aim reticle over your opponent's head.

BUDDY UP

In team game modes, sticking to your teammates is a good idea—foes drop much faster under concentrated fire.

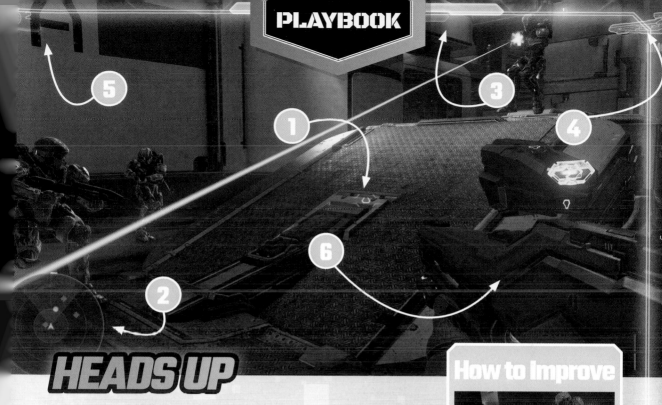

5

1

3

4

6

2

HEADS UP

The *Halo* UI hasn't changed much over the years—it's slick and functional, providing all of the information you require to get ahead in a close-fought match. Even so, FPS games make it easy to focus only on the enemy in front of you. it's a good idea to develop good habits when it comes to checking your minimap, paying attention to your weapon loadout and stock of ammo, and being mindful of the state of the game. Being a great *Halo* player is about more than your aim!

TRY CUSTOM MAPS
Player-made maps can be a great way to practice playstyles.

FORM A TEAM
Regular practice with the same players is very helpful.

PLAY OTHER MODES
You can pick up useful skills playing Firefight or Campaign, too!

1 **RETICLE**
The focus of your aim. Try "dragging" as you shoot for extra accurate fire.

2 **MINIMAP**
Gives you a sense of enemy positions. Get used to checking it every few seconds.

3 **HEALTH AND SHIELD**
Your shield is your best defense, monitor it carefully.

4 **WEAPONS**
You can see your pair of weapons and their ammo counts here.

5 **GRENADES**
Take stock of your grenades— they're great at surprising your foes.

6 **TIMER AND SCORE**
Don't lose track of the match objective!

KEY INFO
Developer: Blizzard Entertainment
Publisher: Blizzard Entertainment
Release date: March 2014
Genre: Collectible Card Game
Play it on: PC, Mac, Android, Apple

HEARTHSTONE

BLIZZARD'S CARD BATTLER!

TAKE A SEAT!

Hearthstone is a digital collectible card game, where two players are pitted against each other with a deck of cards. Each player assumes the role of a legendary *Warcraft* hero from one of nine classes, each with a unique power. Every class can play spells, minions, weapons, secrets, and other powerful cards in an attempt to defeat the other player.

Hearthstone has received tons of expansion packs since its launch, but the game regularly cycles older cards and combos out of competitive play. Pro players have to carefully build decks and adapt to the changing metagame, and plan around the other competitive combinations that their opponents may use. *Hearthstone* is a game of skill and planning, but there's also an element of random chance! As players draw cards and work through their deck, they need to adapt to whatever cards their deck hands them.

Hearthstone is a game that rewards creative, clever players. Building a powerful, effective deck and rolling with the punches of a match is essential in order to claim victory!

⭐ LEARN THESE KEYWORDS

TAUNT
These high-health minions draw enemy attacks to them, forcing your opponent's minions to hit them first! They're very useful for protecting your hero from damage.

SECRET
Secrets are hidden effects that trigger once a certain condition is met. Be careful when you see that "?" on a hero! It means they've got something up their sleeves.

CHARGE
A minion with charge can immediately attack after being placed on the board, rather than a turn later like other units. Watch out for these heavy hitters!

RUSH
Like charge, minions with rush can immediately attack—but they can only target other minions. Rush minions are ideal for clearing out enemy forces when you're in a bad spot.

INSPIRE
These cards will trigger a special effect when a player uses their hero power. They're effective over long periods of time because your hero power is always available to you.

TWINSPELL
Twinspell affects magical spells. When you cast one, a copy will be added to your hand, allowing you to cast it again! Plan ahead to set up devastating spell combinations!

CARD TIPS AND TRICKS

Learn to play your hand, build a deck, and outplay your opponent in *Hearthstone*!

CARD SYNERGY

Cards are designed to synergize together. A mech deck is stronger with other mechs, and a jade druid wants lots of jade idol cards. There's a lot to learn!

POWER CURVE

Packing your deck with high-value minions and spells looks like a good idea, but this leaves you vulnerable in early turns. Make sure you have cards of all levels.

CONTROL THE BOARD

Don't just focus on damage. Sometimes, controlling the board is the better way to win.

GLOSSARY

ZOO
A deck that is filled with a constant supply of minions.

JADE
A deck that relies on jade idols that grow more powerful over time.

TEMPO
The momentum of a match—usually determined by the player in the lead.

CONTROL
A strategy that locks down the opponent and stops their efforts.

WATCH FOR LEGENDARIES

Legendary cards have big effects on the board. Save a card that silences, stuns, or removes these power players for when your opponent plays them.

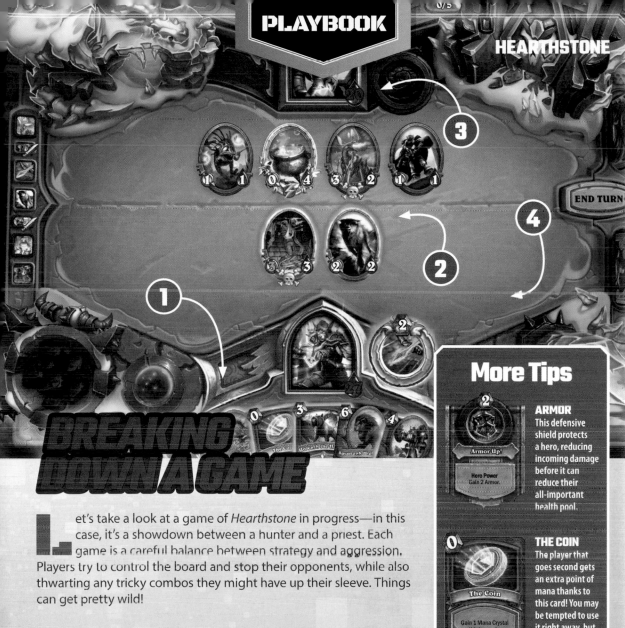

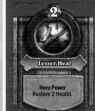

END TURN

BREAKING DOWN A GAME

Let's take a look at a game of *Hearthstone* in progress—in this case, it's a showdown between a hunter and a priest. Each game is a careful balance between strategy and aggression. Players try to control the board and stop their opponents, while also thwarting any tricky combos they might have up their sleeve. Things can get pretty wild!

1 YOUR HAND
These are the cards that you can play this turn, along with their mana costs.

2 MINIONS
This is where each player's forces face off against one another.

3 PORTRAIT
Your opponent's hero, along with their health. Reduce it to zero to win the match!

4 CLICK AROUND!
Hearthstone boards have lots of little secrets to discover—explore to find them!

More Tips

ARMOR
This defensive shield protects a hero, reducing incoming damage before it can reduce their all-important health pool.

Armor Up!
Hero Power
Gain 2 Armor.

THE COIN
The player that goes second gets an extra point of mana thanks to this card! You may be tempted to use it right away, but consider saving it for later.

The Coin
Gain 1 Mana Crystal this turn only.

HERO POWER
Each class has their own special ability, which is designed to be used strategically alongside your hand of cards.

Lesser Heal
Hero Power
Restore 2 Health.

KEY INFO
Developer: Wizards of the Coast
Publisher: Wizards of the Coast
Release date: September 2018
Genre: CCG
Play it on: PC

MAGIC: THE GATHERING ARENA

THE ORIGINAL CARD BATTLER!

WALK THE PLANES!

Magic: The Gathering is the original collectible card game. For almost thirty years, it's ruled the world of tabletop card gaming. Now, thanks to a successful digital version called *Magic: The Gathering Arena*, all of that history is available to enjoy on PC.

Magic is a hugely influential game and most popular CCGs, including *Hearthstone*, were heavily inspired by it. As a result, players of more recent games in the genre will likely find much about *Magic* familiar when they first get started. Don't be fooled, however: All those years of development has honed it into a complex and rewarding strategic sandbox. When you're ready for bigger challenges than *Hearthstone* can throw at you, *Magic*'s where you come. It's the favored hobby of thousands of competitive players for a reason.

It's got a bright future as an esport, too. Physical card game tournaments have been a staple of the *Magic* scene for many years, and its digital incarnation now boasts events with millions of dollars in prizes on the line. The journey to mastering *Magic* is a long one—but there's never been a better time to start!

⭐ CARD TYPES

LAND
Land cards provide mana that is used to cast spells. Most spells require specific types of mana.

CREATURES
Creatures have power and toughness ratings and can be used to launch and block attacks.

SORCERY
When cast, a sorcery has an effect on the battlefield and is then removed from play.

ENCHANTMENTS
Most enchantments are permanent effects that attach to another card.

ARTIFACTS
Unlike enchantments, artifacts do not attach to another card and often come with a cost for use.

PLANESWALKERS
Powerful characters who build and spend loyalty to unleash powerful effects.

FLY YOUR COLORS

Each type of *Magic* card has its own properties—find your own combos!

GREEN

Powerful creatures drawn from nature, along with powers that boost your mana.

WHITE

Favors a defensive playstyle, damage prevention, healing and lots of buffs!

BLUE

Tricks, illusions, and lots of powers that let you draw cards and amass power.

RED

Firepower and aggression! Fling fireballs and summon dragons to the field.

BLACK

Armies of zombies and vampires, and plenty of reasons to sacrifice your own minions.

GLOSSARY

LIBRARY
Magic's word for a player's deck of cards, drawn from at the start of each turn.

INSTANT
Can be played at almost any time, including during your opponent's turn.

PHASE
Part of a turn. Cards take effect in different phases.

PERMANENT
A card or effect that stays on the board until it is removed.

ACROSS THE TABLETOP

There's a lot going on in any game of *Magic*, from the rules on cards themselves to the various ways that players arrange their pieces. In the image above, you can see a typical game of *Magic* in progress.

1 LANDS IN PLAY
You can view each player's lands at the back, so you can see how much mana they have.

2 LIBRARY
Your library grave-yard and exile zone are located in the back corner of the board.

3 PHASES
Here you can see the phases of the game and ask for a pause to play cards at specific points.

4 ATTACKER
This card is attacking, giving the opponent the chance to choose a card to block it.

5 FLYING FOES
Flying creatures can usually only be blocked by other flyers, making them a versatile card.

6 TAPPED CARDS
This card has been tapped, meaning it can't be used until it is "untapped" in the next turn.

Deckbuilding Tips

DON'T FORGET MANA!
Every deck needs plenty of land cards to generate mana. Pack at least 20!

PLAN TO WIN
Don't just stick your rarest cards in a deck —plan your strategy carefully.

PREPARE TO LOSE
You'll inevitably drop a game or two as you hone your deck. Don't get disheartened!

CLASH OF CLANS

FIGHT TO SURVIVE!

KEY INFO
Developer: Supercell
Publisher: Supercell
Release date: August 2012
Genre: Strategy
Play it on: iOS/Android

BATTLE FOR THE CROWN!

Clash of Clans is proof that you don't need a mouse and keyboard to enjoy high-octane, challenging strategy games. From developer Supercell, Clash of Clans is a free-to-play experience designed for mobile devices in which you are tasked with establishing your own town before then working to defend it from other rival players. To do this, players must evolve and upgrade their defenses, which you can only accomplish by raiding other villages. Part of the appeal of Clash of Clans is that you can either do all of this alone or join up with friends and form clans, groups of like-minded mayors eager to shore up their own survival and dominate the game's persistent online servers. While Clash of Clans may look simple on the surface, it's got a surprising amount of depth once you begin to dig a little deeper into it—that's one of the reasons it has become one of the biggest strategy franchises of all time, not to mention one of the most recognizable series the world over.

⭐ TOP TIPS!

STOCK UP
Build as many Gold and Elixir collectors as you can; resource collection is your number one priority if you want to succeed.

COLLECT RESOURCES EFFICIENTLY
Go to the Information tab and divide the rate of collection by the total each can hold, and you'll see how many hours until each collector is full.

FILL SPACE
You need to create a zero-gap base behind those walls you've erected. That way you'll stop any enemies from spawning inside your base.

CLEAR THE LAND
It can be a bit boring, but you should work to clear the 40 random obstacles on your map. Taking these down will earn Gems and XP.

SECURE YOUR MORTAR
No matter the situation, you should secure your Mortar at all costs. Put it in a place that can defend as much of your village as possible!

TRY SINGLE-PLAYER
If you want to earn a little extra in-game cash, you should give the single-player mode a try. Play smart and you'll get a nice little bonus.

CLASH OF CLANS WORLD CHAMPIONSHIP

Want to win one million dollars with just a few frantic taps on your smartphone's screen? Of course you do, it's the dream! Well, now you can. *Clash of Clans* creator Supercell has teamed up with one of the world's biggest competitive production companies—ESL, the Electronic Sports League—to throw a huge Clash of Clans World Championship event. The finals will be hosted in Hamburg, Germany, and will see the six best *Clash of Clans* teams—as well as another two chosen by the community—competing to take home the top prize in a tough-as-nails single elimination tournament. It means you'll only get one chance to prove you're the best. If you ever want to get to this stage, you'll need to get practicing! Find a clan that you like, start investing time into the game every night, and one day you just might find that you're being put onto a plane with your friends to compete in the Clash of Clans World Championship for one million dollars.

ROAD TO FINALS

STRETCHING ACROSS A YEAR, THIS IS THE PATH OF CHAMPS!

▶ **GET QUALIFIED**
Compete in the Champions I League during Spring and Summer.

▶ **PREPARE TO TRAVEL**
The top four clans from the Champions I League battle in 5v5 Offline Qualifiers.

▶ **GO TO POLAND**
The Offline Qualifiers take place in Katowice, Poland. It's a way to meet a fellow clan.

THE BIG LEAGUES

If you ever want to qualify for the Clash of Clans World Championship you'll need to figure out some of the basics first, so keep these in mind as the season progresses and you continue to work toward world domination.

WORK TOGETHER

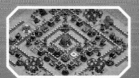

PICK YOUR TEAM

If you want to compete on the global stage, you can't do it alone. What you'll need to do is find four other *Clash of Clans* players that you like to play with and build a solid **team**.

GET LEVELED UP

The first gateway to entry is your level. You'll need to get your Town Hall to level 12 or higher to be able to enter your team into the global competition.

JOIN A CLAN

It's all in the name, isn't it? If you want to succeed you should join a clan and work with the other members of it to secure victory.

USE THE CLAN CASTLE

Your Clan Castle doesn't just signify that you've joined a clan, it's also the unit's main hub of operations. Think of it when you get into trouble.

RESOLVE YOUR WARS

This isn't a case of divide and conquer. Your team needs to be focused on the battles ahead, which means you cannot be in an active clan war to participate.

START FRESH

Given that you can't be in an active clan war, it might be worth creating an entirely new clan with your four teammates just for the purposes of the tournament.

REQUEST TROOPS

If you're really in a bind, don't forget to request help. By doing this, other clan members will send troops to your aid against tough foes.

KNOW YOUR ARMY

Once you're involved in the World Championship you'll find that it moves pretty quickly. That's why you should really spend some time getting to know all of your units.

HAVE FUN!

Sure, winning a lot of money would be great, but the best thing about the Clash of Clans World Championship is the competition itself. Remember to have fun!

BE RESPONSIVE

This is a two-way street of course, so if one of your fellow clan members requests help be sure to send as many troops their way as you can!

▶ PRE-QUALIFIERS

If you miss the Champions I League you can compete in the ESL Clash of Clans Championship.

▶ WORLD CHAMPS

If a clan wins at any of the six Katowice Offline Qualifiers you will be on your way to the World Championship.

FIGHT TO WIN!

Get this far, then you're on the path to win your share of the one million dollar prize pool!

KEY INFO
Developer: Supercell
Publisher: Supercell
Release date: January 2016
Genre: RTS, CCG
Play it on: Mobile

CLASH ROYALE

A CLASH OF CARDS!

ROYALE RUMBLE!

The smash hit *Clash of Clans* became one of the first mobile game phenomenons. Then, developer Supercell took the ideas and characters from that game and decided to create a brand-new, super-streamlined version designed for competitive play. *Clash Royale* was born, and it's been a smash hit since! Players prepare for a one-on-one battle by building decks of cards that represent units. In a match, players must send their units marching toward their opponents to destroy their enemy's towers.

The best part? It all takes place in real time, against anyone in the world—no waiting for your turn!

Because *Clash Royale* allows players to take each other on, of course a competitive scene quickly appeared. Supercell was fast to support it, too. Now, the company holds international tournaments, and top esports organizations send their players out to see who's the best at this mobile sensation. Unlike many esports games, *Clash Royale* tournaments are open to anyone—maybe you could be the next *Clash* champion!

DID YOU KNOW?

Clash Royale held the largest esports tournament in the world in 2017, with 27 million players participating online from around the world!

⭐ COMMON CARDS

SKELETON
The weakest but cheapest card—send plenty out to distract enemy units!

PRINCE
A simple but efficient card to beat down a tower or large enemy.

BABY DRAGON
Fly above enemy troops and take them down with a fireball!

KNIGHT
This beefy guy has a sturdy balance of both attack and health.

GOBLIN
Three goblins shoot arrows for a cheap elixir cost!

HOG RIDER
These madcap marauders ride straight for the enemy tower!

CLASH, DON'T CRASH!

Keep these tips in mind to keep your towers standing and earn crowns!

MANAGE RESOURCES

Elixir can disappear before you know it! This is most obvious when you're using heavy hitters, but elixir can vanish when you use too many smaller cards also. Watch your gauge!

WIN MORE, BUILD MORE

Gold is the currency with which you buy and upgrade cards. It can be earned from winning battles—which, of course, is good practice anyway.

DON'T RUSH TOO FAST

Using many cards at once seems good, but you'll not only run out of cards, your enemy may find a way around (or through) them all!

BALANCE YOUR DECK

Don't have too many weak cards, but don't stack your deck with big hitters! Including a wide range of cards means you're prepared for almost any situation.

GLOSSARY

TROOPS
Basic marching attack units, from weak skeletons to powerful wizards!

SPELLS
Cards with special effects that deal damage or provide boosts.

BUILDINGS
Stationary units that deal damage or generate troops.

RARITY
How difficult it is to find a card to add to your decks. Rarity is power!

LEAK ELIXIR WISELY

When you earn 10 Elixir but don't use a card, you "leak" elixir—and can't earn any more to use. This isn't always bad, but don't make it a habit!

BEST-LAID PLANS

So you've decided to step up onto the battlefield. Maybe you've built a perfect deck for yourself, or you're raring to give your new cards a try. That means it's time to test your nerve against a real opponent! *Clash Royale* pits you against an opponent in real time, which can be a daunting prospect—it's one thing to come up with a great plan, but another thing to pull it off!

The standard battlefield has a consistent, simple layout. All around it, there are visual cues about what cards you can use, who's winning, and how long your units are going to last on the battlefield. Paying attention to these can be key to an incredible play—or claiming victory!

1 PRINCESS TOWER
Taking it down awards a crown!

2 KING TOWER
Destroying this is an instant win!

3 ELIXIR
Spend this to summon troops to the field!

4 CARDS
The cards you're currently able to play.

5 NEXT CARD
Drawn when you next use a card.

6 CROWNS
Earn three crowns and you win the game.

Deck Strategies

BRIDGE SPAM
Keep the enemy at bay and creep your way in!

BEATDOWN
Send out the big troops, but don't get caught by spells!

TRIPLE SPELL
Taking three spells leaves no room for troops, so play smart!

GETTING INVOLVED

START YOUR COMPETITIVE GAMING JOURNEY!

Now that you've read up about the biggest games in competitive gaming, there's a good chance that you're chomping at the bit to begin your own competitive journey. That's great! There are lots of ways to get involved in playing games competitively no matter how old you are, where you live, or what types of games you're passionate about. Over the following pages, we're going to show you how to pick your game, foster a competitive attitude, find opportunities to play, and form a winning team. Honing your skills and meeting new friends is highly rewarding—we're sure you're in for an exciting journey!

WARMING UP

First up, the big question: Why become a competitive gamer? After all, honing your skills takes dedication—there's much more to it than simply playing more of your favorite game—and very few players get to lift a trophy without lots of hard work. Everybody dreams of chasing the big prize, but the very nature of competition means that only a handful of players get to claim titles for themselves. Every player, however, gets to benefit from the journey itself.

The rewards for getting involved in competitive play are very similar to regular sports. This is a way to meet other people who share your passion, and to find a community that understands your favorite game in the way that you do: There's something special about the secret language that seems to form between devotees of a particular sport.

It's also an opportunity to develop vital skills like teamwork, discipline, and problem solving, and you'll carry these with you wherever your passions take you next, whether that's the next big game, education, or a future job. Esports build confidence, teamwork, and communication. And who knows—with a little luck and hard work, you could join the elite group of players who are able to rise to the top!

DID YOU KNOW?
Many pro players start competing at a young age, but it takes dedication and discipline to get to that point!

PICK YOUR GAME

SUPER SMASH BROS. ULTIMATE
Nintendo's epic brawler is a competitive hit with a thriving community and lots of events.

LEAGUE OF LEGENDS
Riot's all-conquering MOBA has a highly professional esports scene with lots of opportunities to advance.

POKÉMON
Competition is in Pokémon's DNA, and every year there are major events to compete in.

ROCKET LEAGUE
A relative newcomer, *Rocket League* has proven to be a smash hit with esports players.

THE RIGHT STUFF

Get into the competitive spirit with these vital skills!

LEARN TO LOSE

Everybody loses—even winners! It's a part of competitive life, so you've got to learn to enjoy playing whatever the result—and to be glad when a setback provides you with new lessons to learn!

PRACTICE SKILLS

Every game features tricks and techniques that form the building blocks of success. Taking time to practice in friendly games or against the computer can really pay off.

SEEK CRITIQUE

There's always something to learn from other players. Ask your competitors or teammates to point out what you could be doing better, and take their suggestions to heart!

BALANCE IN ALL THINGS

Although practice is important, you've got to approach it in a balanced way. Exercise and a healthy lifestyle are vital if you want to reach your potential.

TEAMWORK TIPS

FORM A WINNING SQUAD

FRIENDS FIRST

Great teams support each other both in-game and out of it. Share your successes and rise up together—you're better as a unit!

LEAD FAIRLY

Even if you're the captain, everybody's voice is important. Make sure you give everybody an opportunity to make suggestions.

TALK IT UP

Communication is key—and takes practice. Work on ways to quickly make in-game calls and be responsive to your teammates.

TRY EVERY IDEA

Teammates don't always agree about the best strategies, but don't be afraid to try out new ideas—you may be surprised by what works!

JUNKRAT
200 / 200

ESPORTS AT SCHOOL

CLUBS, SUMMER PROGRAMS, AND MORE

Although many esports players have found success at a relatively young age, it can be tricky to find opportunities to find teams, hone your competitive skills, and enter tournaments when you're just starting out—particularly if you're not yet old enough to attend some of the larger events or enter online competitions.

High school esports programs provide one potential solution! All over the world, school esports are popping up—along with after-school events and summer programs that help connect all of these individual clubs into a growing community. In many cases, these clubs work just like any other school society, like tabletop gaming, anime, or robotics. Players meet up to discuss and enjoy their favorite games, form teams, and compete against other clubs—winning glory for their schools in the process! Many game developers directly endorse school and youth leagues, meaning that club play can be a gateway to the wider world of esports. Even where those

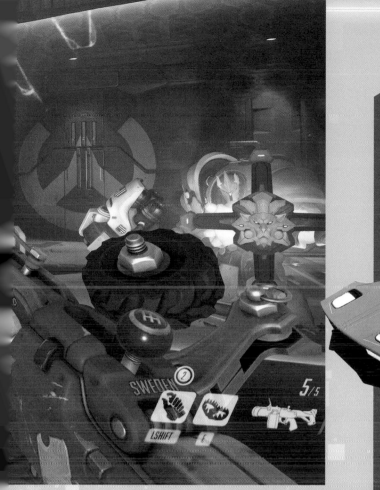

Q&A

connections don't yet exist, it's a way to gain valuable experience and opportunities to attend events in person.

So how do you get involved? The first step is to find out if your school has an esports club of its own. If not, the High School Esports League (highschoolesportsleague.com) and NASEF (esportsfed.org) are great resources for gamers in the USA. Their websites have information and resources to help you go about setting up your own club, and have lots of useful advice that can help you even if you live elsewhere in the world.

As for what comes next, many colleges now have varsity esports programs—your school esports league could lead naturally to the next step in your education!

WHAT GAMES DO SCHOOL CLUBS PLAY?

There are lots of options, but games like *Overwatch*, *League of Legends*, and *Rocket League* have proved particularly popular thanks to their focus on teamwork and coordination.

WHAT KIND OF EVENTS COULD I GO TO?

School club tournaments are chiefly held online, but opportunities to take to the stage with your club team do exist—including the League of Legends High School Invitational, which takes place during their College League of Legends Championship.

I DON'T LIVE IN THE USA—CAN I STILL FORM A SCHOOL CLUB?

The answer is almost always yes! Various organizations provide support for school clubs elsewhere in the world. The British Esports Organization, for example, provides lots of information for budding players in the UK.

ROAD TO THE TOP

START

CAN YOU REACH THE TOP OF THE GAME?

1

FIND YOUR GAME

You may already know what your game of choice is, but think ahead—does it have a thriving competitive scene? Are there major teams or esports organizations involved? What kind of viewing numbers is it pulling in on YouTube or Twitch? All of these factors play a role in making an esport viable.

2

3

GET COMPETITIVE

As your training continues, you'll want to start competing—either in online leagues, or leaderboards or at events. There's no substitute for practice under pressure, and real competitions—even if the stakes aren't very high at first—will make you more confident and capable, win or lose.

12

11

10

13

14

BIGGER EVENTS

With wins come access to bigger, better events and bigger, better prizes. At this point, you've got to prove that you're not a flash-in-the-pan. Continue to be successful as the stakes rise and you'll draw the attention of orgs and audiences alike.

15

FINISH

BECOME A PRO!

You've bagged yourself a team, a contract with an esports organizations, and a bucketload of wins—you've done it! Welcome to the big leagues: Your journey to the pros is complete. Reaching the very top, however? That's going to take even more dedication—and plenty of challengers stand in your way!

23

22

4

LEARN FROM THE BEST

When you've settled on a game, it's time to study. Watch pro matches and replays to assess how the performance of the best players in the world differs from your own. You'll undoubtedly have a lot to improve, but learning from the best is a great way to know where to start!

5

6

PRACTICE SMART

Balance training with school, exercise, rest, nutrition, and other essentials. There's no use mastering a game if you're not able to access those skills when it counts, and a balanced lifestyle is essential in order to reach the top—it's what separates pro players from merely skilled ones.

8

8

BOOST YOUR ATTITUDE

As your skills develop, so should your competitive attitude. That might mean working on your teamwork, or it could mean figuring out how to take criticism —everybody has something they need to overcome as they become more dedicated to their esport of choice. It's what's inside that counts!

7

16

GET RESULTS

That said, this is the road to the top — so results matter. Making a name for yourself through victories is essential if you want to progress, but it doesn't need to happen overnight. If you don't do well in your first tournaments, it's time for more practice —or a change in approach.

17

18

FIND A TEAM OR ORG

It's at this point that you'll want to start seriously considering whether esports could be a career—and if it is, then the support of a professional team or esports organization is always helpful. Different games have different structures, but getting scouted at an event is a major career milestone.

21

20

19

RUNNING YOUR OWN TOURNAMENT

EXPERIENCE THE THRILL OF COMPETITION AT HOME!

Even if esports glory feels like a distant dream, it's always fun to compete. Friendly competitions let you and your friends show off your skills in the comfort of your own home, and can provide valuable experience of the pressures of competition—even if the stakes aren't very high! If you're an aspiring esports events organizer, setting up an event for your friends could be a fun way to get used to tournament structures, recording results, and organizing round after round of play. Home tournaments can be played in an afternoon or play out over several weekends, league-style—there's no wrong way to do it!

PICKING THE

STREET FIGHTER V

For decades, fighting games like *Street Fighter* have been a staple of friendly competitions both at home and in the arcades. If you've got a group of friends who really know their stuff, a *Street Fighter V* game can be a great way to bond over favorite characters and techniques. Even if you're new to the game, learning through friendly competition is a great way to develop a passion for one of the most legendary fighters ever.

SUPER SMASH BROS. ULTIMATE

It's no accident that *Smash Bros.* is such a fan favorite. Its flexible competitive structure makes it uniquely good for tournament organizers of all kinds. It supports one-on-one play, multicharacter battles, and team games, as well as various degrees of seriousness, from item-free contests of pure skill to powerup-fueled party game madness. If in doubt about what game to pick, *Super Smash Bros. Ultimate* is a reliable hit.

ROCKET LEAGUE

Playable both in splitscreen and online, one-on-one or with teams, *Rocket League* is another versatile pick. Because it combines arcade-style car controls with the fundamentals of soccer, it's also pretty easy for new players to wrap their head around—even though it's a tough game to master! There's tons of depth for your players to explore, too, both in terms of individual skill and teamwork.

POKÉMON

Pokémon is all about building and training your own team of creatures, and that naturally lends itself to friendly competition. Almost every version of the game supports multiplayer battles via system link, and this makes it a great choice for a school league or tournament—just create a way for players to set up matches and you're on the way to building your very own Elite Four!

RIGHT GAME

CHOOSING THE RIGHT TITLE FOR YOUR EVENT OR LEAGUE!

MARIO KART 8 DELUXE

Although it's not regarded as an esports game, very little beats *Mario Kart* when it comes to split-screen console action. The Switch's multiplayer functionality makes it particularly good for setting up tournaments on the go, and *Mario Kart 8 Deluxe* is the perfect game because it's relatively easy for new players to pick up. This is an ideal choice if you're catering to a big group of gamers with varied tastes.

MAGIC: THE GATHERING ARENA

Magic's long history as a tabletop tournament favorite makes it a solid choice for your own competitions. Although *Magic: The Gathering Arena* exclusively supports online play, you could easily set up a league for you and your friends to participate in. If you're part of a *Magic: The Gathering* club at your school or in your hometown, then it'll be easy to find players to round out your new league!

MINECRAFT

Minecraft's a great choice because it provides so many ways to play. There are loads of competitive minigames to dig into, and any or all of them could support a home league. But there's also different forms of competition, like build battles—why not see which of your friends can put together the most spectacular build, or create something with a time limit? It's a very different but equally valid way to compete!

FORTNITE

Fortnite can be tricky to incorporate into a home tournament or league simply because it's played online against a hundred other players—but that doesn't make it impossible! Why not set up a league where you and your friends record your results in online matches and compete to become the most consistent winner? That'd be a great way to establish yourself as a local *Fortnite* expert!

FINDING YOUR

MATCH TYPES

While some gaming contests take the form of a single match, the majority are played in a best of three, best of five, or best of seven format. This means that the overall winner is determined by their performance across several games against the same opponent—after the specified number of rounds, the team with the most victories is the winner! The advantage of this format is it prevents one fluke result from determining the outcome. Also, in games that involve changing team compositions or different maps, having to play multiple rounds ensures that players are tested in lots of different competitive circumstances.

DID YOU KNOW?

Team Liquid are the only team in history to win the *Dota 2* International grand finals without losing a single game!

BEST OF THREE

PLAYER ONE   PLAYER TWO

V

V

V

PLAYER ONE WINS!

FORMAT

THERE'S LOTS OF WAYS TO RUN A TOURNAMENT!

BRACKET TYPES

Lots of tournaments and leagues end with some kind of bracket—a system where teams face off and eliminate each other with the winners of each round progressing until the two best teams meet in the final. In a single elimination bracket, a single loss is enough to see a participant knocked out—it's a fairly brutal way to compete, with high stakes attached to each game. However, it's pretty fast to run! In double elimination brackets, teams that lose a game enter a "lower bracket" and face off against other teams as they get knocked down. Keep winning in the lower bracket and you'll eveunally get a chance to play your way back into the final—you need to lose twice to get knocked out.

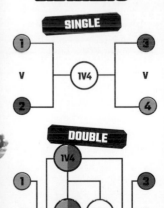

ELIMINATION BRACKETS

SINGLE

1
3
V — 1V4 — V
2
4

DOUBLE

1V4
1
3
V — 3V4 — 1V3 — V
2
4
2V3

ROUND ROBINS

Round robin is a comprehensive way to rank all of the players in a competitive field, and can be adapted to work as both an event format and a league format depending on the number of participants and the game. In a round robin, every participant plays every other participant one after another, and then they're ranked by how many wins they picked up over the course of the competition. In the event of a tie, other factors like points scored or number of wins in each best of three can be used to establish rank.

The downside of a round robin is that it can take a very long time, making it suitable for long-running leagues but tough to do in a day. Also, it can create situations where it's impossible for participants to catch up with the player or team in the lead, which can be pretty disheartening!

P1 V P2

P3 V P4

P2 V P3

P4 V P1

P1 V P3

P2 V P4